# Orwell

# Orwell

Scott Lucas

HAUS PUBLISHING · LONDON

First published in Great Britain in 2003 by
Haus Publishing Limited
32 Store Street
London WC1E 7BS

Copyright © Scott Lucas, 2003

The moral right of the author has been asserted

A CIP catalogue record for this book
is available from the British Library

ISBN 1-904341-33-0 (paperback)

Designed and typeset in Albertina at Libanus Press, Marlborough

Printed and bound by Graphicom in Vicenza, Italy

Front cover: photograph of George Orwell courtesy of University
College, London
Back cover: painting of George Orwell by Peter Blake

# Contents

# Introduction

Like many Americans of my generation, my acquaintance with George Orwell was limited. There were the obligatory encounters with *Animal Farm*'s pigs and the rats of *1984* (American texts have always used, incorrectly, the numerical form of the title), but nothing of Orwell's other novels. The required anthology for my university class, 'Creative Writing 101', featured 'Why I Write' and 'Politics and the English Language', but there was no mention of his numerous essays, the newspaper columns, or the literary criticism. In many ways there was no need, for Orwell's two novels and his writer's manifesto were sufficient to establish the man and his meaning. In a world threatened by the menaces of communism and postmodernism, here was the sanctuary of political, moral and aesthetic 'clarity'.

This reassuring image was undisturbed for almost a decade. Then, while researching an article on propaganda in the Cold War, I found a reference to a meeting between George Orwell and an official of the British intelligence services. I had stumbled into the rumour, known only by a few biographers and conspiracy theorists, that Orwell had been co-operating with Big Brother even as he was denouncing him. Three years later, rumour became 'fact' with the belated release of government papers and the encyclopaedic work of Peter Davison.[1] Orwell had compiled a notebook of 105 individuals suspected of links with the Soviet Union, or of communist tendencies, or of 'impure thoughts'. He had not only met with a British official, but had passed on 36 names to the intelligence services.

Had it not been for a sentence in an obscure memorandum, my 'Orwell' would have remained an unchallenged guide to the consistency and decency of the crystal spirit. Once Orwell's contact, some might say collaboration, with the 'grey' propagandists of His Majesty's Government was confirmed, simple image gave way to a full re-evaluation. I was not satisfied, as Orwell's defenders were, with passing off the incident as an anomaly, a 'party game', the hasty act of a feverish, dying man, a knee-jerk reaction to Reds under British beds.

Given the opportunity to consider the entire scope of Orwell's life and work, decency and the 'free' intellectual gave way to a far more complex character. Orwell the author, as opposed to 'Orwell' the creation of biographers, philosophers of 'liberalism' and politicians, was no longer consistent, no longer complete, no longer guaranteed to be objective and rational. Indeed, if there was a constancy in Orwell's writing and views, it was not in a 'positive' sense. He changed, often rapidly, from a declared conservative to an 'intellectual anarchist', to an independent socialist, to a pacifist, to an anti-pacifist patriot, to the defender of anti-Soviet Englishness, to a free liberal.

Instead, Orwell was always buttressed by a 'negative' caricature of the enemy that he was confronting. In his earliest books and essays, the foe was the general environment of imperialism or a material culture that devalued humanity. By 1935, he was beginning to identify a more substantial opponent and, perhaps surprisingly, it was not an establishment 'right' that had defined Britain's capitalist empire. Rather, the menace was from those supposedly alongside Orwell: the Socialist activists of *The Road to Wigan Pier* (1937); the *pansy poets* and left-wing editors of *Homage to Catalonia* (1938); the intellectuals *sniggering . . . at patriotism and physical courage* of *The Lion and the Unicorn* (1941),[2] these same intellectuals under *the poisonous effect of the Russian mythos* of his essays after 1945.[3] Orwell's note-book was simply the private record of a very public animosity.

I do not hope in this book to offer a definitive portrait of Orwell. Nor do I wish to deny or erase his significant influence, often for good, in political, economic and social movements from his time to ours. I only hope to put the opinion that Orwell was far too complex a man to be reduced, either by himself or by others, to an icon of 'decency' and a guide to be followed in all cases of past or present uncertainty.

I am writing this in a hotel room overlooking the Ramblas in Barcelona. The city still has the power to entrance, just as it captured Orwell's imagination 65 years ago as *a town where the working class was in the saddle*. Yet with its life, dynamic yet relaxed, of street performers, stalls selling flowers, newspapers and all sorts of pets, shell-game artists, and with its arguments, its romances, and even its processions of students singing and dancing in fancy dress, it is far from the *gaunt, untidy* Barcelona of 1936.[4]

The Café Moka, which was the Civil Guard headquarters observed by Orwell from the rooftop across the Ramblas, now has a shiny steel frontage and larger-than-life photographs of young people smiling giddily over its offerings. The agonies of the Civil War have not been forgotten, but Spain has survived Franco and is now a prominent member of an expanding European Union. Catalan flags fly outside the hotels and Barcelona and Madrid consider each other uneasily, most notably on the football pitch; however, the prevailing atmosphere is one of growth. Concerns are elsewhere: the front pages of the newspapers announce that the United Nations has adopted a resolution to send weapons inspectors into Iraq, though analysts still expect the US to press for regime change in Baghdad.

A half-century after his death, the world has moved beyond

Orwell, even beyond the Cold War that framed his final achievement. Yet 'Orwell' is still constructed and placed before us. In October 2001, Michael Kelly, the prominent US columnist challenged any scepticism over the bombing of Afghanistan with the remark: 'The American pacifists . . . are on the side of future mass murders of Americans. They are objectively pro-terrorist . . . That is the pacifists' position, and it is evil.'[5] His inspiration for the comment was a 1942 contribution to an American periodical by George Orwell about pacifist dissent over the conduct of war with Germany.

Last year, Christopher Hitchens, a self-styled successor to Orwell, wrote: 'I sometimes feel as if George Orwell requires extricating from a pile of saccharine tablets and moist hankies.'[6] Surely, if we were to pursue the ideal of independent thought, 'Orwell' does not need to be rescued for us. Rather, we need to rescue ourselves from 'Orwell'.

The Blair Family, 1916: Parents – Ida Mabel and Richard Walmesley Blair with children Marjorie and Eric

# Origins

The story begins simply. On 25 June 1903, in the town of Motihari in the province of Bengal in British-ruled India, Eric Blair was born.

But then things get complicated. For Eric Blair would never become famous until he adopted the pseudonym 'George Orwell', and 'George Orwell', born in the Asian subcontinent, became an English, arguably *the* English writer of the 20th century. The champion of the 'common man' would have a far from common existence: while his family was not exactly wealthy, his origins in the white-collar bureaucracy of the empire led to an early life in public schools and foreign postings far removed from the working class.

It is in the tale of this journey from Eric Blair to 'George Orwell' that the author's ultimate success, as well as his possible failings, might be found. For all the talk of absolutes such as freedom, truth and clarity in his life and work, 'George Orwell' is a construction. He was created by Blair, first to guard against the fear of failure, then as a persona to represent independence and the virtues of *good prose . . . like a window pane.*[7] The process did not end, however, with Blair's death in January 1950. Instead, over the past half-century, others have created their own Orwells for their own intellectual, political and social ends.

Eric Arthur Blair was the second child and only son of Richard Blair, an official in the Opium Department of the Indian Civil Service, and Ida Limouzin Blair, the daughter of an English mother and a French father who frittered away the family's businesses in Burma. Richard Blair was 46 when his son was born; his wife was 28.

Eric's childhood was soon marked by disruption. When his father took up a new post in a large Indian town, Ida took the children to Henley-on-Thames in Oxfordshire. Between 1904 and 1911, Richard Blair would only see his family for three months during leave in 1907. Even after retirement and return to England, he preferred gardening and golf to spending time with his son. In 1917, he joined the British Army in France, supervising the care of mules and then working at the Ministry of Pensions before retiring for good at the end of 1919. Later, he would resolutely oppose his son's decision to leave the Indian Imperial Police for a career as a writer. Only in the last days before his death in 1939 did he finally express his approval of 'George Orwell'.

Ida Blair was not unsettled by her husband's absence. To the contrary, she seems to have preferred independence and detachment. When they were together, she made it clear through her condescension and a considerable degree of authority who actually ran the family home. As one relative observed of Richard Blair: 'Poor old Dick. If he was heard poking the fire it was "Dick, put that poker down".'[8]

Many biographers of Eric Blair have speculated on the psychological effects of what was effectively a one-parent family. George Orwell would produce mixed memories of the years in Henley, which became a model for the idyllic countryside of his protagonist in *Coming Up for Air* (1939). He had few friends, but he was an avid reader and his mother encouraged his first attempts at writing. *I wrote my first poem at the age of four or five*, he claimed some 40 years later, *my mother taking it down to dictation. I cannot remember anything about it except that it was a tiger and the tiger had 'chair-like teeth' – a good enough, phrase, but I fancy the poem was a plagiarism of Blake's 'Tiger, Tiger'.*[9]

On the other hand, Orwell repeatedly painted a bleaker picture

of his mother, such as when she forbade him from playing with
a neighbour's children because *they were common*. In his memory,
the resulting loneliness, as much as his mother's encouragement,
produced his eventual triumph: *I knew that I had a facility with words
and a power of facing unpleasant facts, and I felt that this created a sort of
private world in which I could get my own back for my failure in everyday life.*[10]

These memories are not a consistent basis for considering
Orwell's work. They can be convenient anecdotes, as in Orwell's
epiphany that it was class prejudices that had prevented him playing with *common* children. In other cases, they need to be carefully
unpacked. Eric's life with his mother did not result in a particular
closeness in later years or in special fondness for women in his
novels and documentaries. Orwell's recollection of disconcerting
conversations between his mother and her friends about *the
hatefulness — above all the physical unattractiveness — of men* prompts

speculation that the author exacted masculine revenge with female characters who were vain, grasping or abusive.

Blair/Orwell's attitude to women – in his fiction and his reportage, in fantasy and in 'real' life – has provoked bitter critical disputes. In later years, he was not especially close to his mother and was careful to leave the impression that she gave him a combative image of male–female relations, recalling his boyhood impression that *women did not like men, that they looked upon them as a sort of large, ugly, smelly and ridiculous animal who maltreated women in every way, above all by forcing their attentions upon them.*[11]

Other women in Blair's family are absent from Orwell's recollections. Although his aunt and grandmother lived in Burma, where Blair served in the 1920s, he never referred to them. Eric did have a close relationship with his sister's friend, Jacintha Buddicom, which continued throughout his teenage years, but the image Orwell left of his young adulthood was one in which women were beyond love, if not conquest. Much later he would speak wistfully of the sweetness of Burmese women[12] and would reminisce with male friends about the wonders of sex in public parks.

Orwell's richest, if not fondest childhood memories revolve around his stay at St Cyprian's, the Sussex preparatory school that he joined at the age of eight. In 1947, he completed a long essay, 'Such, Such Were the Joys', with the declaration: *The real question is whether it is still normal for a schoolchild to live for years amid irrational terrors and lunatic misunderstandings.*[13] This memoir was so provocative and potentially libellous that it was not published in Britain until the early 1960s.[14] Orwell's St Cyprian's was run by a malevolent headmaster and his even more intimidating, arguably sadistic, wife. Both were more concerned about keeping order than the welfare of the boys; in the graphic opening scene of the essay, Orwell recounts his humiliation when the headmaster's wife told a stranger of his bed-wetting and threatened to have him beaten for the offence.

Orwell's most protective biographer, Bernard Crick, has struggled to soften this portrayal of St Cyprian's by referring to Eric's letters to his mother and landmarks such as the publication of his first poem in a local newspaper. 'There is no evidence of disturbance,' notes Crick. 'A child in terror would write more briefly and in safe and easy stock phrases, not so chattily and spontaneously.'[15] The point, however, is not the contemporary 'truth', but Orwell's perception of his schooldays from the 1930s to the end of his life. As he wrote to his friend Cyril Connolly: *It's all like an awful nightmare to me.*[16] His description of a third-rate public school in *A Clergyman's Daughter* (1935) is

Cyril Connolly (1903–74) reviewed for the *Sunday Times* for many years. In 1939, he founded *Horizon*, the influential literary magazine, with the poet and critic Stephen Spender (1909–95). His only novel is *The Rock Pool* (1936) but he is also remembered for *Enemies of Promise* (1938), an amusing exploration of the pitfalls of literary success, and *The Unquiet Grave* (1944), a collection of aphorisms and reflections written under the pseudonym 'Palinurus'.

drawn from the deep well of his animosity, and after the Second World War he would castigate the British government for failing to abolish privately-funded education. The contented schoolboy Eric, if he ever existed, was long gone.

Conversely, psychological readings of Orwell (such as those of Anthony West) have played up the bleakness and hostility of St Cyprian's as a major inspiration for *Nineteen Eighty-four* (1949).[17] Did a prep school inspire the dystopia of Oceania's London, the helpless Eric becoming the oppressed Winston Smith? Orwell may have drawn upon his schoolboy anxieties, but this analysis risks simplification. St Cyprian's was not to be the only period of desolation and pain in his life.

After a short stay at another school, in 1917 Eric received a scholarship to attend Eton, the archetypal English public school. Despite the institution's tradition of beatings in the first year, his correspondence indicates a satisfaction with school life. However, because he was 'a bit of a slacker and a dodger',[18] his academic results were poor. The silver lining, according to the legend of the making of 'George Orwell', was his extracurricular reading: the American novelist Jack London (1876–1916); the playwright and freethinker George Bernard Shaw (1856–1950); the father of science fiction H G Wells (1866–1946); the poet of nostalgia and 'lost content' A E Housman (1859–1936); and the rebellious Romantic poet Percy Bysshe Shelley (1792–1822).

Eric's school record is mundane and intriguing at the same time. He started a magazine, *Election Times*, but the poems he contributed were not diamonds in the rough. More interesting was his very un-Orwellian stance as both *a snob and a revolutionary* at Eton.[19] 'George Orwell' might condemn organised sports *as bound up with hatred, jealousy, boastfulness, disregard of all rules and sadistic pleasure in witnessing violence,*[20] but Eric Blair put great effort into football and the famous Wall Game (a form of football played

Before an Eton Wall Game, 1921 (Eric Blair on far right of back row)

at Eton). Orwell would criticise organised religion, but Eric Blair was confirmed in the Church of England.

Orwell, sceptical about wars for nationalism, recalled that at Eton, *the war had almost ceased to affect us.* He continued: *In the school library, a huge map of the Western Front was pinned on an easel, with a red silk thread running across on a zigzag of drawing pins. Occasionally the thread moved half an inch this way or that, each movement meaning a pyramid of corpses. I paid no attention.*[21] Still, if his schoolboy enthusiasm for the war had abated (his first published poem had called for volunteers and praised the military hero Lord Kitchener), Blair was no pacifist. He displayed 'a more positive although certain sardonic' liking for the compulsory service in the Officers Training Corps and took charge of the Signals Corps with a touch of youthful rebelliousness.[22]

To note the differences between man and boy is not to accuse Orwell of deceit or even inconsistency. Rare is the individual whose opinions at 18 will last for life. At the same time, the notion can be dispelled that 'George Orwell' – saint or sinner – emerged full-blown as the young Eric Blair.

Blair's lack of academic achievement ruled out certain paths. No scholarship to Oxbridge was forthcoming, and there was no consideration of a 'lesser' university. A lucrative or prestigious job evaded him. Instead, Blair took the exams of the India Office for admission to the Imperial Police. He passed, despite a poor riding test, and in October 1922 sailed for Burma as a probationary Assistant Superintendent.

Blair's five years in Burma were distinguished by their lack of distinction. He moved often, taking up seven posts and, after initial training, never staying longer than nine months in any one location. He was competent, but he was not regarded as a 'high flyer' by his superiors, and he was uncomfortable among the expatriate community. By 1927, he had had enough. Recovering from dengue fever, a painful and debilitating disease, Blair was

George Orwell's application papers to join the Burma Police, 1922. Orwell (Eric Blair) served in the Burma police from 1922 to 1927. The experience inspired his first novel, *Burmese Days*, published in 1934.

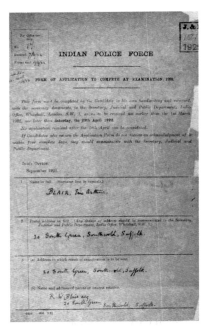

Burma Provincial Police Training School, Mandalay, 1923. (Eric Blair standing third from left)

granted permission to spend sick leave in Britain. He never returned to Asia.

Some scholars have tried to find the birth of 'George Orwell' in Burma. Eric Blair, serving in the heart of the world's largest empire, undergoes an epiphany and opposes imperialism. However, Blair's Burmese observations and jottings are more concerned with personal turmoil than an emerging political awareness. Much later, 'George Orwell' would admit that his earlier incarnation was far from radical, recalling how Eric Blair used copies of the left-wing journal the *Adelphi* for target practice. His concerns, at least in unpublished poems and a few sketches that appeared later in *Burmese Days* (1934), were of a tortured young man struggling between base idealism and his even baser instincts:

The *Adelphi* was started in 1923 as a monthly journal edited by John Middleton Murry (1889–1957). As the *Adelphi* or the *New Adelphi* (1927–30) it ran until 1955 and included among its contributors the poets W B Yeats (1865–1939), T S Eliot (1888–1965), Cecil Day Lewis (1904–72) and W H Auden (1907–73), and the novelists Arnold Bennett (1867–1931), H G Wells and Orwell.

### ROMANCE

When I was young and had no sense
In far-off Mandalay
I lost my heart to a Burmese girl
As lovely as the day.

Her skin was gold, her hair was jet,
Her teeth were ivory;
I said, 'For twenty silver pieces,
Maiden, sleep with me.'

She looked at me, so pure, so sad,
The loveliest thing alive,
And in her lisping, virgin voice,
Stood out for twenty-five.[23]

So it was that, after a stopover in southern France, Eric Blair came home. *I was already half determined to throw up my job,* Orwell later wrote, *and one sniff of English air decided me.*[24] But the Englishman would not succeed in England yet. He struggled with his sketches; as a friend, Ruth Pitter, recalled: 'He wrote so badly. He had to teach himself writing. He was like a cow with a musket . . . We used to laugh 'til we cried at some of the bits he showed us.'[25] Blair spent more and more time (as his boyhood literary hero Jack London had done) meeting tramps and beggars in the East End of London, eventually spending several nights in lodging houses and 'spikes'[26] on the outskirts of the city.

In spring 1928, to become a writer, Eric Blair left the English air behind to make a name for himself in Paris.

# Wanderings

*Down and Out in Paris and London* was published in January 1933, and in the five years it took him to write it, Eric Blair became 'George Orwell'. Nevertheless, if it is a political book, it remains uncertain what kind of awakening had occurred.

Blair had not set out to examine poverty by leading an impoverished life. For more than a year, he lived in a shabby but far from intolerable area of the Latin Quarter, seeking the novel that would make his reputation. He hoped to finance himself (as well as to establish his name) by writing articles, the first of which appeared in December 1928. For G K Chesterton's *G.K.'s Weekly* he dissected the French right-wing press, and he described British unemployment for the French newspaper *Le Progrès civique*. Three more contributions to *Le Progrès* followed, notably a study of British imperialism in Burma.

A homeless person wrapped up against London's cold

In his articles, Blair defined what he was against. He was launching his polemic against tabloid, mass-market journalism, a righteous hatred that would recur in his novels and essays: *Every paper of this kind, whatever its intentions, is the enemy of free speech.*[27] He was beginning to criticise the British empire that he had only recently served, and he was introducing the observations of deprivation and inequality that would distinguish *Down and Out in Paris and London*. Yet nowhere in his articles would Blair set out what he was *for*, other than, presumably, some alternative to the status quo. This was observation rather than analysis or argument.

Blair's existence in Paris as a journalist was over almost as soon as it began. In early 1929, he was hospitalised with pneumonia, the beginning of his lifelong battle with pulmonary illness. Then, in the summer, he was forced into a struggle for survival after his money was stolen by a woman he had picked up in a café. (In *Down and Out* she is turned into an Italian thief.)

The latter catastrophe was the catalyst for Blair's authorial breakthrough, forcing him into an extended experience of poverty. He cut his expenditure to the minimum necessary for food and shelter, pawned his clothes, and spent many hours looking for the most menial jobs. Eventually, with the help of a Russian acquaintance, he found work as a *plongeur*: washing dishes and carrying out minor chores in a hotel kitchen. For financial security, he worked 14 hours a day. Just before Christmas 1929, Blair accepted the failure of his initial plans and returned to Britain. He took a job caring for a mentally-impaired boy in Southwold, the coastal village in Suffolk where his parents now lived.

But there may have been more to the prodigal's return. A few weeks earlier, the *Adelphi*, which Blair had formerly used as a target, became his patron when it agreed to publish his article on being a tramp in London, 'The Spike'. More acceptances followed, and Blair visited the journal's offices, describing 'himself as a Tory anarchist but admitt[ing] the *Adelphi*'s socialist case on moral grounds'.[28]

'The Spike' was notable mainly for the pattern it set for his early writing, serving as the basis for two chapters of *Down and*

*Out* and for various characters in *A Clergyman's Daughter*.[29] (A related essay, 'Hop-Picking', appeared in the *New Statesman*, but was a toned-down version of Blair's notebook observations.)[30] the *Adelphi* also featured 'A Hanging', a far more powerful piece than his reportage from Paris or London. The description of the pathos and horror of an everyday execution in Burma was not explicitly political, but the essay skilfully conveyed Blair's distaste with both British authority and the local population. He juxtaposed the serious and the mundane with the closing anecdote of a group's laughter as six warders pulled on the legs of the condemned to get him out of his cell: *We all had a drink together, native and European alike, quite amicably. The dead man was a hundred yards away.*[31]

The impact of 'A Hanging' was a singular exception, however, and Blair struggled to sell his first book-length work, 'A Scullion's Diary', based on his life in Paris. Meanwhile he was working as a part-time tutor, travelling with the hop-pickers in Essex, and sometimes living rough in London, farcically attempting to get arrested on one occasion so that he could experience Christmas in prison. He fought to survive, writing a friend in October 1931: *I am getting stories etc to do for the new paper* Modern Youth. (*A poisonous name for a poisonous paper — & the things I write for them are also poisonous, but one must live.*)[32] Even this opportunity ended in failure; *Modern Youth* folded before the stories were published and Blair could be paid.

It was here that the *Adelphi* connection meant far more to Blair than publications and income. The co-editor, Sir Richard Rees, with a baronetcy and an assured private income, became a close friend. Initially, Rees was not an enthusiastic supporter of this new contributor, who was 'intelligent and able', but not 'especially original or gifted', though he noted that Blair was not prone to 'the jealous, pushful, intriguing, self-centred mentality which is so common among young ambitious literary men'.[33] He lent money to Blair and introduced him to other writers and publishers. After the publisher

Jonathan Cape rejected *Down and Out*, Rees recommended it to T S Eliot at Faber and Faber.

'We did find [the manuscript] of very great interest,' replied Eliot, 'but I regret to say that it does not appear to me possible as a publishing venture.'[34] Defeated, Blair handed the chapters to a friend, saying: *Throw them away but keep the paper clips.*[35] Instead she made a decision that led to the birth of 'George Orwell': she took *Down and Out* to a literary agent, Leonard Moore. Moore, who would represent Blair for the rest of his life, sent the manuscript to the left-wing publishing house of Victor Gollancz in August 1932. Gollancz found it 'an extraordinarily forceful and socially important document'.[36]

The title *Down and Out in Paris and London* was only agreed upon at the last minute (*Confessions of a Dishwasher* was another possibility). There was further drama over the name of the author. In April 1932, Blair asked his agent to *see that [Down and Out] is published pseudonymously, as I am not proud of it.*[37] Seven months later he came up with some suggestions: *A name I always use when tramping etc. is P S Burton but if you don't think this sounds a probable kind of name, what about Kenneth Miles, George Orwell, H Lewis Allways? I rather favour George Orwell.*[38]

Sir Victor Gollancz (1893–1967) founded his own publishing house in 1928, and the Left Book Club in 1936. He was well known for his progressive views and his resistance to Fascism.

Orwell was the name of a local river south of the Blair home at Southwold, but there is no explanation for 'George' other than the fact that Blair hated his first name: *It took me nearly 30 years to work off the effects of being called Eric.*[39] Gollancz, who had previously suggested the less-than-imaginative 'X', agreed immediately to the name.

The financial returns from *Down and Out* were modest, but the reviews in leading newspapers and journals were more than encouraging. The *Times Literary Supplement* hailed it as 'a vivid picture of an apparently mad world'. Cecil Day Lewis (1904–72, the future Poet Laureate, commended the book's 'clarity and good sense', and the novelist J B Priestley (1894–1984) praised it as a 'social document of some value' and 'the best book of its kind that I have read in a long time'.[40] In the US, where Moore soon arranged publication, most reviewers repeated the compliments: James Farrell wrote, 'Orwell has escaped from the depths. There are thousands to whom no door of escape is opened. *Down and Out in Paris and London* will give readers a sense of what life means to these thousands.'[41]

Orwell's ability, not only to observe but to bring those observations to life, had finally emerged in his 'unique and strange information'.[42] The book's vivid depiction of settings and characters and its crisp use of language is apparent from the opening paragraph: *The rue du Coq d'Or, Paris, seven in the morning. A succession of furious, choking yells from the street. Madame Monce, who kept the little hotel opposite mine, had come out on to the pavement to address a lodger on the third floor. Her bare feet were stuck into sabots and her grey hair was streaming down.*[43] At the heart of the Paris section, the naturalism is even more intense as Orwell takes the reader down into the *stifling, low-ceilinged inferno of a cellar* where he washes dishes.[44]

The account of Orwell's tramping in England is less intense, but just as well observed. Orwell takes us into his confidence as he descends into the lower classes, transforming himself into the

A soupline in Paris

lowest of the low. When he first swaps his clothes for some old rags, he shares his shock with the reader: *I had worn bad enough things before, but nothing at all like these; they were not merely dirty and shapeless, they had – how is one to express it? – a gracelessness, a patina of antique filth, quite different from mere shabbiness.*[45] The change of pace and tone is deliberate and effective: whereas Orwell is an obvious 'alien' in France, his alienation in England, among his fellow countrymen, is portrayed as a kind of revelation. Conversely, Orwell's unlikely (given his own background) bonding with his fellow down-and-outs is neatly realised, as when the tramps obtain a cup of tea by pretending to pray in a tin-roofed mission hut: *We knelt down among the dirty teacups and began to mumble that we had left undone those things that we ought to have done, and done those things that we ought not to have done, and there was no health in us.*[46]

Much of the power of *Down and Out* comes from its being 'true'. In fact, Orwell took artistic liberties with his story, such as the mysterious, quite fictional benefactor who rescues him from France. Similarly, the explanation for Orwell being down-and-out in London is that his carer's job in Suffolk had been delayed for a month; the incident is contrived to incorporate his tramping into the plot. For a friend, Orwell annotated a first edition of the book: *Succeeding chapters not actually autobiography, but drawn from what I have seen.*[47]

The issue of the 'authenticity' (or otherwise) of Orwell's account encourages his biographers to play detective, but it is of little significance. Bernard Crick's fervent examination and defence of the author is beside the point,[48] for *Down and Out* is ultimately a triumph of the personal rather than the political. As the periodical *Time and Tide* noted: 'It is not only George Orwell's experiences that are interesting; George Orwell himself is of interest.'[23]

Orwell's description of his descent into squalor may be vivid, but it is not designed to bring any reaction beyond a gasp of 'Isn't this terrible?' As the author noted simply in the introduction to the French edition: *The basic theme is poverty.*[50] The book is not intended as a critique of the political or economic system that has produced such widespread poverty. In fact, the only political presence in the book is the *Communist secret society*, but this enemy within turns out to be a group of swindlers taking money from Russian refugees.

Orwell limits any argument he is making with a specific, if not distorted, notion of poverty. The declaration of an *everyday experience* of deprivation is contrasted with the exceptional existence in Montmartre, where Orwell encounters deviant raconteurs in bars, hangs out with exotic foreigners, and participates on the margins of the cultural mélange that is Paris in the late 1920s. As Crick observes, these are not the faces of the majority who have always been poor but of middle-class characters that have fallen.

In the end, Orwell is the outsider who is 'rescued' not by any fundamental change in his political and social environment but either by providence or by his middle-class connections, which permit him to choose when to end his impoverished existence. The people he encounters in Paris and London are abandoned, most of them lacking Orwell's mysterious benefactor to return them to society. As an American reviewer noted, shrewdly if perhaps unfairly: '[Orwell has] colored the facts a little . . . One reads on with a sort of horrid fascination, happy in the suspicion (eventually verified) that this existence in the gutter is but the temporary condition of a man who rather enjoys being down and out.'[51] The *Manchester*

*Guardian*'s praise, in the first published review of the book, is worthy but hyperbolic: '[Orwell has] so much to say in that quiet, level voice of his that he has written a book which might work a revolution in the minds of those who are totally unable to look on down-and-outs as other than something entirely unlike themselves.'[52]

To be fair, Orwell never claimed that *Down and Out* was the start of a political pilgrimage. Instead it was a very long apprenticeship in his quest to be a novelist.[53] His impressive powers of observation were being honed and developed not in order to expose the workings of the 'system', but to give his fiction a greater sense of realism.

Encouraged by the imminent appearance of *Down and Out*, Orwell raced ahead with the first chapters of the long-planned but previously aborted *Burmese Days*. He was fretful, writing to Leonard Moore: *I know that as it stands it is fearful from a literary point of view, but I wanted to know whether given a proper polishing up, exclusion of prolixities and general tightening up, it was at all the sort of thing people want to read about.*[54] Fortunately, he received reassurance, telling a friend, *The agent was very pleased with the 100 pp. of my novel I sent him and harries me to get on with it.*[55]

Still, becoming a novelist was far from uncomplicated. With his parents surprised and even a little disapproving of his venture and a secure income far from guaranteed, in April 1932, Orwell took a teaching position at a small private school in Hayes, west London. He loathed the job, but at least the holidays gave him time to write.

There was one other diversion. Blair was pursuing his first serious courtship, romancing a family acquaintance named Eleanor Jaques. Later, passages in *Keep the Aspidistra Flying* (1936) and *Nineteen Eighty-four* would draw upon Blair's desperate efforts to woo Eleanor, made fraught by her simultaneous relationship with Dennis Collings, soon to be an official in the British Colonial Service. *It is such lovely weather and it would be so delightful to go for a long walk in the country somewhere,* wrote Blair. *If you can't manage a Saturday or Sunday, I can always make an excuse & get away. Or at worst we could meet in town for an afternoon.*[56] Protracted planning appears to have led to the occasional pastoral rendezvous, but the battle was lost in 1934 when Eleanor married Collings.

We can only speculate how much Orwell's fretting, and the apparent competition with another suitor for Eleanor, contributed to John Flory's romantic travails in *Burmese Days.* Orwell completed the draft in December

Orwell in 1932

1933, though he submitted it only because he was *sick of the sight of it.*[57] Nevertheless, a more prosaic problem emerged. The publisher, Victor Gollancz, feared the novel would provoke lawsuits from colonial administrators who recognised themselves in the characters. Orwell's American publishers, Harper's, signed a contract in March 1934, but *Burmese Days,* delayed while Harper's legal advisors looked it over, did not appear until October. Gollancz finally published a British edition in June 1935, after several names in the text had been changed.

The extended negotiations over publication hindered the promotion of *Burmese Days.* Though some reviews praised a 'superior' or 'admirable' novel,[58] most were limited to a description of the plot. Sales were moderate. The book's anticlimactic appearance, along with Orwell's self-deprecation, meant that *Burmese Days* has never received the attention, or indeed devotion, given to some of his other works.

*Burmese Days* deserves our attention because it is Orwell's attempt at a 'naturalist' novel, which also provides a far-from-simple representation of British imperialism. His methodical description is served well by a Burmese jungle which, in contrast to much of his London, is vibrant and full of colour. Of course, the brightness is not necessarily positive – the jungle can bring danger as well as release from the banal existence of British club life.

The physical environment is juxtaposed and intersects with a social environment with its own threats. The characters in Flory's club may be two-dimensional portrayals of racism, corruption and superficial manners, but Orwell perfectly conveys the corrosion of power casually assumed as imperial right and vigorously asserted as racial superiority. He is less successful with his depiction of the Burmese, divided into evil local magistrates, lackey servants, petulant mistresses, and everyone else as an unthinking mob. Only the portrait of Dr Veraswami, Flory's best friend who occupied an uncertain position – excluded from the local population because he is Indian, excluded from the British community because he is *black* – goes beyond the usual rendering of the 'other' side.

In contrast to the personal account of *Down and Out*, the 'fictional' *Burmese Days* offers a complex political vision of oppressor and oppressed. However, its complexity is not an unmitigated blessing. Flory ends up dead, Veraswami ruined, and Orwell in a muddle. The issue is not just the ascendancy of melodrama in the text, with the stilted rise and fall of the relationship between Flory and Elizabeth Lackersteen (who, far from incidentally, is the first of Orwell's treacherous female leads). Any gesture of Flory's anti-imperialism will be indecisive and futile because he will always be an outsider. He cannot be part of the British community that he despises, but nor can he ally himself with the Burmese people who, in his eyes, are corrupt, gold-digging or savage. Most are simply *unknowable* beyond their appearance, and those whom Flory comes to know he neither likes nor respects.

While it is usually an error to equate the opinions of a novel's protagonist with those of its author, Orwell offers supporting evidence that Flory the outsider is, in fact, a fictional embodiment of Eric Blair/George Orwell, an outsider in Burma and still an outsider on his return to England. One suspects that the elevation of a doomed romance in the text occurs in part because of Flory's lack of self-confidence – a combination of paralysing fear of 'superior' women, disdain for 'common' females, and an idealised notion of 'romance' – a striking parallel for Orwell's own stumbling, immature approach.

More to the point, politically, Orwell (like Flory) is a conflicted anti-imperialist. As the cultural theorist Raymond Williams shrewdly observed: 'He was at once opposed to the dirty work of imperialism and involved in it.'[59] In a kinder spirit, the critic Malcolm Muggeridge labelled Orwell 'more Kiplingesque than Marxist'.[60] Orwell's 1929 reportage in *Le Progrès civique* had identified *despotism . . . in a mask of democracy*[61] and in 'A Hanging' he had documented the destruction of *a healthy, conscious man;*[62] however, these texts, like *Burmese Days*, are susceptible to the charge that they do not sufficiently question the racism of imperial expansion.[63]

'Shooting the Elephant', Orwell's sharpest essay on the imperial situation, maintains this ambivalence. Its power is captured in Orwell's frank admission: *With one part of my mind I thought of the British Raj as an unbreakable tyranny, as something clamped down . . . upon the will of prostrate peoples; with another part I thought that the greatest joy in the world would be to drive a bayonet into a Buddhist priest's guts.*[64] British power is abusive when it can be exercised, farcical when it cannot. Yet the Burmese are ignorant, incapable of ruling themselves and susceptible to the manipulations of a few local representatives. The status of victim cannot confer autonomy.

Orwell may be arguing that imperialism is corrosive because it

Mohandas Karamchand 'Mahatma' Gandhi (1869–1948) was the spiritual father of Indian independence. Educated in London, he worked in South Africa before returning to India in 1914 where he became leader of the Indian National Congress Party and advocated a policy of peaceful non-cooperation and civil disobedience. After numerous periods of imprisonment, he negotiated India's independence in 1947. He was assassinated by a Hindu fanatic the following year.

Jawaharlal 'Pandit' Nehru (1889–1964) was a follower of Gandhi and President of the Indian National Congress. After Indian independence, he was India's first prime minister.

grinds down the colonised, but in 'Shooting the Elephant' he also grants the slaves a paradoxical, manipulative power over their masters: *It is the condition of* [the British man's] *rule that he shall spend his life in trying to impress the 'natives', and so in every crisis he has got to do what the 'natives' expect of him.*[65] There were, however, leaders among the oppressed. Orwell's approach in *Burmese Days* had been to caricature them as corrupt and venal; in his non-fiction of the 1930s, he never recognised them. Only in 1942 would he begin to consider the nationalist movement in India and, when he did, it was with little respect and a good dose of vitriol: *Gandhi is deliberately making trouble . . . impossible to be quite sure what his game is.*[66] Nehru's question 'Who dies if India lives?' brought Orwell's retort: *How impressed the pinks will be.*[67]

Moreover, from 1936, Orwell began to waver in his castigation of imperialism. In 'On Kipling's Death' (1936), Orwell's affection for Kipling resulted in a vision of the empire that verges on the rose-tinted: *The imperialism of the 'eighties and 'nineties was sentimental, ignorant, and dangerous, but it was not entirely despicable . . . It was still possible to be an imperialist and a gentleman, and of Kipling's personal decency there can be no doubt.*[68]

Orwell's ideological position was being curbed by his literary preferences − Kipling had been a favourite author of the schoolboy Blair − and would soon be bound by more pressing political objectives. During Orwell's pacifist phase of 1938−9, his criticism of empire was sharp: *When you see how people live, and still more how easily they die, it is always difficult to believe that you are walking among human beings. All colonial empires are in reality founded upon that fact.* Orwell was still portraying the 'natives' as somehow subhuman −

Rudyard Kipling (1865–1936) was the first English writer to receive the Nobel Prize (1907), but his reputation as the poet of the British empire led to accusations of jingoism, vulgarity and racism (he coined the phrase 'the white man's burden'). His least controversial works are *The Jungle Book* (1894), and *Just So Stories* (1902), and his best novel is *Kim* (1901). His poem, 'If', remains popular today.

observing Senegalese soldiers was *almost like watching a flock of cattle* − but he was also exposing the truth that every white coloniser must have been thinking: *How long can we go on kidding these people?*[69]

In 'Not Counting Niggers', published two months before the outbreak of the Second World War, Orwell took the argument as far as he could. He did so, however, not by targeting the traditional defenders of imperialism, but by assailing his new foes on the 'left'. Accepting the fact that British prosperity rested upon the economic resources of its colonies, Orwell argued that the British socialists calling for the independence of those colonies must be hypocrites: *The majority of left-wing politicians and publicists are people who earn their living by demanding something that they don't generally want.* They wanted to take Britain into war against Hitler, not for freedom and self-determination, but *to stabilise something that is far bigger and in its different way just as bad.*[70]

Two years later, Orwell the pacifist had become Orwell the patriot, and his attitude towards imperialism was adjusted accordingly. Ostensibly calling for the independence of India, he framed this in the context of *pansy-left* critics who misinterpreted Kipling and an Anglo-Indian ruling class who deserved at least a modicum of redemption: *It may be that all that* [Anglo-Indians] *did was evil, but they changed the face of the earth.*[71] As for the 'natives', Orwell complained that *the Indian intellectuals in* [Britain] *go out of their way to antagonise those likeliest to help them.*[72]

For the rest of his life, the anti-imperialism of *Burmese Days* took second place to Orwell's other priorities. In January 1949, in his last completed essay, he softened his earlier criticism of Gandhi and praised his *natural physical courage,* his freedom *from that maniacal suspiciousness which . . . is the besetting Indian vice,* and his belief in the good faith and good nature of all people. In the end, though, the man could not match up to the requirements of the Cold War: *There is reason to think that Gandhi . . . did not understand the nature of totalitarianism . . . It is difficult to see how Gandhi's methods could be applied in a country where opponents of the regime disappear in the middle of the night and are never heard of again . . . Is there a Gandhi in Russia at this moment? And if there is, what is he accomplishing?*[73]

All these complexities lay ahead of Orwell, who was intent on becoming a 'writer' even though he once wrote: *Never start writing novels, if you wish to preserve your happiness.*[74] While finishing the manuscript of *Burmese Days,* he was publishing four poems in the *Adelphi,* the best returning to the observation of *Down and Out: A dressed man and naked man . . . Bargaining for a deal; Naked skin for empty skin, Clothes against a meal.*[75]

Days after completing the novel, he contracted pneumonia when he was caught in a downpour during a long motorcycle ride. Initially, doctors feared for his life, but as soon as the danger had passed Orwell was hard at work on his next project. With his mother urging him to recuperate in the parental home in Suffolk, he could temporarily give up teaching and concentrate on writing *A Clergyman's Daughter*.

The novel begins with a unique twist for Orwell: his protagonist is a woman. The life of Dorothy Hare, caught up in the routine of village life and service for her father and his church, changes dramatically when an amnesiac episode leads her to subsistence in the countryside and on the streets of London. There is a further inter-

> *One result of the breakdown of religious belief has been a sloppy idealisation of the physical side of life.*
>
> GEORGE ORWELL, November 1935

lude as a teacher at a poorly-run girls' school. Dorothy turns adversity to promise with innovative methods that motivate previously uninspired pupils, but she is undone by their parents' insistence on *practical work, not all this fancy stuff* and a rigid and hypocritical morality, which forbids her to mention the word 'womb' in *Macbeth*.[76] She returns to drudgery in the vicarage.

*A Clergyman's Daughter* is usually regarded as Orwell's weakest novel. The innovation of a female viewpoint is short-lived; Dorothy Hare is 'George Orwell' in a dress. The scenes of hop-picking and roughing it are pallid. Having brought the down-and-out to readers through his essays and documentaries, Orwell had gone to the well once too often. The author and critic V S Pritchett noted Orwell's proficiency at satire, but added that the novel too often fell into 'the glib cruelties of caricature'. Others thought the text 'ambitious yet not successful' or commented that the 'sure and bold' approach and 'often brilliant' dialogue was hindered by a plot that was 'neither new nor convincing'.[77]

The repetition of the narrative rests uneasily with Orwell's attempted structural innovations. He had been re-reading James Joyce's *Ulysses*, smuggling in a copy from abroad to avoid the British censors. He concluded in depression: *When I read a book like that and then come back to my own work, I feel like a eunuch who has taken a course*

Irish novelist James Joyce (1882–1941) is best known for *Dubliners* (1914), a book of short stories which includes 'The Dead', one òf the finest stories ever written; *A Portrait of the Artist as a Young Man* (1914–15), an autobiographical novel; *Ulysses* (1922), regarded by many as the greatest novel of the 20th century; and *Finnegans Wake* (1939), a beautiful but uncategorisable work of linguistic experimentation.

*in voice production and can pass himself off fairly well as a bass or baritone, but if you listen closely you can hear the good old squeak just the same as ever.*[78] Ultimately, as V S Pritchett realised, Orwell's 'immense knowledge of low life, its miseries, humours, and talk' was overshadowed by a '"stunt" Joyce fashion that utterly ruins the effect'.[79]

As he read Joyce, Orwell complained that his own novel, *instead of going forwards, goes backwards with the most alarming speed. There are whole wads of it that are so awful that I really don't know what to do with them.*[80] Passages such as the Trafalgar Square scene are indeed the weaker siblings of Joyce's depictions. Orwell, again racing to finish a draft, admitted to Leonard Moore: *It was a good idea, but I am afraid I have made a muck of it . . . The book does . . . contain an inherent fault of structure* [but] *this could not be rectified in any way that I can think of.*[81]

While trying to craft a novel distinct in its structure and style, Orwell had left behind his powers of observation. *A Clergyman's Daughter* peters out in simplistic assertions. Life in provincial England is often mundane and boring. Being a clergyman's daughter can be a difficult life. Dynamic teachers are thwarted by school management and parents. And, once again, there are many impoverished or itinerant people whom you may never have encountered or, having encountered them, never really thought about. That's about it.

Orwell could console himself that Victor Gollancz had eagerly accepted the manuscript, that Harper's had given him a nice advance for the American edition of *Burmese Days*, and that he had a new job in a London bookshop, with lodging in a room above the premises. He had also begun a relationship with Kay Welton, an aspiring poet who owned a secretarial agency.

Orwell still hadn't established his literary credentials, so he redoubled his efforts. He drew up a strict schedule for himself: *7am get up, dress etc. cook & eat breakfast. 8.45 go down & open the shop, & I am usually kept there till about 9.45. Then come home, do out my room, light the fire etc. 10.30–1pm I do some writing. 1 pm get lunch & eat it. 2pm–6.30 pm I am at the shop. Then I come home, get my supper, do the washing up & after that sometimes do about an hour's work.*[82] He began work on a verse epic of the history of the English people and a novel about a struggling poet working in a London bookshop. The former was abandoned to appear only as a humorous reference in the plot of the latter, his third novel *Keep the Aspidistra Flying*.

The protagonist, Gordon Comstock, is yet another incarnation of the author. Like Orwell, he rails against the literary cliques that are blocking the recognition of his talent. Like Orwell, he sneers at the materialism of London, contrasting its false colour with its real drabness. Like Orwell, he pines for a relationship, but panics about the costs of lifelong commitment, children and a mortgage.

This closeness to the author was criticised by reviewers, particularly as the plot of Gordon's descent into desperation is rather stilted. Yet Gordon is an effective channel for Orwell's polemics. And in Rosemary, Gordon's long-suffering girlfriend, Orwell created the only female character in his work who is not a cliché or a natural threat to men. She earns our sympathy rather than our derision.

For Orwell does not make Gordon likeable. He is self-absorbed, boorish and insensitive (all, by extension, aspects of Orwell). The reader might identify with Gordon's sense of being trapped in the *money society*, but the scene where Gordon, having overcome his immediate financial difficulties and loss of self-esteem through a $50 payment by an American journal for one of his poems, spends the windfall in drunken, insulting debauchery is so painful that emotions are divided once more. The ambivalence is heightened because of the unquestioned goodness of those surrounding Gordon, including Rosemary, the millionaire socialist Ravelston, and Gordon's sister Jenny.

There is further ambiguity in the target of Gordon's diatribes. His rantings against the materialism of London are directed not against economic or political masters but against the manifestations of mass culture, such as the disregard for quality literature, posters for 'Vitamalt' and 'Bovex', or *those desolate hotels which exist all along the motor roads and are frequented by stockbrokers airing their whores on Sunday afternoons.*[83] This, however, is hardly a socialist tract. Gordon is not concerned with a detailed examination of the political and economic processes of the 1930s that have contributed to widespread unhappiness and even despair, only with the symptoms that supposedly make *his* life an urban hell.

The resolution of the novel is also far from straightforward. Gordon, eschewing Rosemary's offered sacrifice of an abortion, accepts her preferred option of a job with an advertising agency, an apartment with the iconic aspidistra, and marriage; in short, all the trappings of the commodified existence he loathes. Yet, because Rosemary is so good, shouldn't we also accept this as the best conclusion?

Some critics have fallen into the trap and contended that Gordon makes his peace with the money society, even though only the most strained reading could produce evidence of Gordon's contentment. The best that can be said is that he has finally reached a moral line – the abortion of his child – that he will not cross for the sake of his personal battle and his dreams. Gordon – like Flory in *Burmese Days* and 'George Orwell' in *Down and Out* – can choose either self-destruction or a subsistence that he does not welcome.

For the 'political' Orwell, the most important feature of the novel may not have been Gordon's capitulation at all, but the alternative that Gordon closes off. Orwell mocks socialism in his portrayal of Gordon's benefactor, the hereditary millionaire Ravelston, who publishes the 'leftist' journal *Antichrist*. When he enters Ravelston's flat, Gordon is immediately on his guard: *There was something in the atmosphere of the flat that upset him and made him feel mean, dirty, and out of place. It was so overwhelmingly, though unconsciously upper-class.* As Orwell, the omniscient narrator, explains: *The truth was that in every moment of* [Ravelston's] *life he was apologizing, tacitly, for the largeness of his income.* And he reminds the reader: *No rich man ever succeeds in disguising himself as a poor man; for money, like murder, will out.*[84]

Ravelston is particularly notable because he was based on Orwell's friend, Sir Richard Rees. Having featured the author's early work in the *Adelphi*, Rees continued to open doors for Orwell's literary and political development. When Orwell was researching *The Road to Wigan Pier* in early 1936, he carried letters of introduction from Rees to political and social activists. Through Rees, Orwell made the initial connections that would take him to fight in Spain, and it was at an *Adelphi* summer school that Orwell proclaimed his conversion to socialism.

The issue is not that Orwell was a 'bad' socialist. He had not settled on any political philosophy or affiliation; as his fellow lodger, the writer and journalist Jon Kimche, put it, Orwell was 'a

By the age of 22, Sir Richard Rees (1900–70) was honorary attaché at the British Embassy in Germany and had succeeded to his father's title as second baronet. Yet, within three years, he was appointed 'honorary treasurer and lecturer' of the Workers' Educational Association in London. After six years as editor of the *Adelphi*, he worked in a Spanish hospital during the Civil War and served in the British and French navies in the Second World War, earning the Croix de Guerre. Besides writing several books, he exhibited at the Royal Academy and translated the essays and letters of the French philosopher and mystic Simone Weil (1909–43).

kind of intellectual anarchist'.[85] Just as he had done in *Down and Out*, Orwell was still defining what he was *against*. He might not like the new class system brought about by the new consumer culture, but he would not join any organised opposition to it.

As Orwell was drafting *Keep the Aspidistra Flying*, he wrote to a friend about an illuminating incident. Repeating the storyline of Gordon and Ravelston, he had gone to Rees's flat to borrow money, but learned that his benefactor was at a socialist meeting.

Orwell followed and recalled: *I spent three hours with seven or eight Socialists harrying me, including a South Wales miner who told me – quite good-naturedly, however – that if he were a dictator he would have me shot immediately.*[86]

Orwell was caught up in a literary career that was productive but limited. The mixed reactions to *A Clergyman's Daughter* had been followed by criticism, much of it hostile, of the 'crude' *Keep the Aspidistra Flying*. 'The obsession with money,' observed Cyril Connolly, 'is one which must prevent [the book] from achieving the proportion of a work of art.' Compton Mackenzie in the *Daily Mail* began with praise, but then warned that Orwell may have reached the limit of his ability: 'No realistic writer of today has produced books of greater vigour and reality. But among the aspidistra, Mr Orwell seems to lose touch with reality . . . There is some searching talk, and one or two ideas are given an airing which, though not strictly fresh, will pass as original.

A novel, however, needs something more than this.'[87]

Was this a premature end? The demands of getting by when one *was half starved and had to turn out something to bring in £100 or so* meant that Orwell could not afford the time to refine and develop his *silly potboilers*.[88] He was unlikely to succeed with innovations in style or structure, and there was a question of the life-cycle of his strident critiques of the everyday. He confided to a friend in 1934: *Everything is going badly. My novel about Burma made me spew when I saw it in print, & I would have rewritten large chunks of it, only that costs money and means delay as well. As for the novel I am now completing [A Clergyman's Daughter], it makes me spew even worse, & yet there are some decent passages in it.*[89]

Orwell was not down and out, but he looked like a man with nowhere to go.

# Home and Away

At the start of 1936, two events altered the course of Orwell's career. The first was that his quest for love and marriage, almost as relentless as the demand to write, finally succeeded. At a party he threw in London in spring 1935, he met Eileen O'Shaughnessy, a graduate student in psychology. Within three weeks, he had proposed to her; she refrained from accepting, but only until she had completed her degree and earned some money. The prospect of marital bliss did not displace Orwell's fears (*by next year we may all have been blown sky-high*),[90] but by his wedding day, on 8 June 1936, he could consider a fresh start. He took time out from ceremony and celebration to write a friend: *I have had a bloody life a good deal of the time but in some ways an interesting one.*[91]

The match was not idyllic. Orwell continued to see other girlfriends – despite his declaration after first meeting her that *Eileen O'Shaughnessy is the girl I want to marry*[92] – and there would be tensions and affairs throughout the marriage; however, the relationship with Eileen checked Orwell's pessimism about his life and his work. It also focused his intellectual energies. Eileen Blair was intelligent, firm in her opinions, and engaging in her comments. Although she did not belong to a political organisation, she was interested in current affairs and espoused a general 'socialism'.

The second turning point was Victor Gollancz's suggestion (supported by the offer of a £500 advance) that Orwell should write about workers and the unemployed in the cities of northern

Eileen Maud O'Shaughnessy is the 'lost' figure from the legend of George Orwell. Before she met him, she had been a teacher and the owner of a successful secretarial agency, but she gave up business to pursue a Master's degree in educational psychology. She suspended her studies when she married Orwell, but her correspondence and the testimonies of friends reveal a woman of insight with strongly held opinions and the ability to express them clearly.

England. From January to March 1936, Orwell stayed with working-class families and in ill-kempt lodging houses, including one above a tripe shop. He interviewed people in their homes, crawled through coal mines, consulted official reports in public libraries and attended political talks. By May, he was converting the material into *The Road to Wigan Pier*.

It was the first time Orwell had travelled north of London, and the effect was to take his observation out of the run into which his 'English' essays and novels had fallen. With a fresh eye, he could render the everyday exotic: *The earth is so vast and still so empty that even in the filthy heart of civilisation you find fields where the grass is green instead of grey; perhaps if you looked for them you might even find streams with live fish in them instead of salmon tins. For quite a long time, perhaps another 20 minutes, the train was rolling through open country before the villa-civilisation began to close in upon us again, and then the outer slums, and then the slag-heaps, belching chimneys, blast-furnaces, canals, and gasometers of another industrial town.*[93]

Orwell also displayed a new dimension and depth in his description of poverty. He drew extensively from his stays with a variety of landlords and hosts, and from adventures such as his descent into a coal mine. More importantly, he used statistical data for the first time, carrying out the research in Wigan's public library. Orwell was not only describing deprivation but proving it with empirical calculations and assessment: *There are great numbers of people who are in work but who, from a financial point of view, might equally well be unemployed, because they are not drawing anything that can be described as a living wage. Allow for these and their dependants, throw in as before the old-age pensioners, the destitute, and other nondescripts, and you get an underfed population of well over ten million.*[94]

*The Road to Wigan Pier* exposes the inequality and the futility of much of 'working class' life. A 1979 study by Peter Stansky and William Abrahams put the case eloquently: 'In those seven chapters [are] a portrait of poverty and its consequences that catches at the imagination and awakens sympathy and anger, even now, some 40 years later, when the appalling conditions it describes have long since been ameliorated – perhaps, in some slight degree, as a consequence of the book itself.'[95] Even Orwell, after cautiously writing, *I am afraid I have made rather a muck of parts of it*, was *fairly pleased* with the outcome.[96] Days after he submitted the manuscript in December 1936, Gollancz asked him if the documentary could be a selection for the Left Book Club, which had been created for readers 'who desire to play an intelligent part in the struggle *for* World Peace and a better social and economic order, and *against* Fascism'.[97] The decision ensured a wide circulation among subscribers; more than 40,000 copies of the first edition were sold, and the book was reprinted twice.

The educational aim of the Left Book Club (founded in 1936 by Victor Gollancz) was to resist the rise of fascism and Nazism. It flourished as a movement, circulating political books to some 50,000 members. The Club was dissolved in 1948.

Nevertheless, Orwell had reached a troublesome impasse at the end of Part One of his book. He had effectively documented the contemporary problem, but there was no way he could prescribe a cure beyond the vague injunction to bring *an effective Socialist party into existence.*[98] He had neither the ability nor the inclination to do so, as he had admitted on his return from Burma: *I had at that time no interest in Socialism or any other economic theory. It seemed to me then – it sometimes seems to me now, for that matter – that economic injustice will stop the moment we want it to stop, and no sooner, and if we genuinely want it to stop the method adopted hardly matters.*[99]

In the years that followed, he had made no advance on this position. Orwell had no knowledge of the economist Adam Smith, or of Karl Marx, or of J M Keynes, whose *General Theory of Unemployment, Interest and Money* appeared in 1936. Orwell brought no history to the book; the recent cataclysms of the First World War (1914–18), the General Strike (1926), and the fall of the Labour government (1931) are equally absent. No alternative vision of Orwell's England appears, because no other vision is evaluated or even cited. As the economist and political philosopher Harold Laski observed, Orwell's 'socialist propaganda . . . ignores all that is implied in the urgent reality of class antagonisms. It refuses to confront the grave problem of the State. It has no sense of the historic movement of the economic process.'[100] More than 30 years later, Raymond Williams noted that 'Orwell hated what he saw of the consequences of capitalism, but he was never able to see it, fully, as an economic and political *system*.'[101]

Orwell did not have to be more of an 'intellectual' to make *The*

The Scottish economist Adam Smith (1723–90) is best known for *An Inquiry into the Nature and Causes of the Wealth of Nations* (1776), the first serious work of political economy. In it he prophesied that America would be 'one of the foremost nations of the world'.

German philosopher, economist and revolutionary Karl Marx (1818–83) was the founder of modern international communism. His extreme, radical views forced him to spend much of his life in exile. In Paris, he met Friedrich Engels (1820–95), with whom he wrote *The Communist Manifesto* (1848). The following year he moved to London, where he worked on his masterpiece, *Das Kapital* (Vol. 1, 1867), a critique of the capitalist system.

NO SOLUTIONS

One of the most influential economists of the 20th century, John Maynard Keynes (1883–1946) revolutionised economic approaches to handling recession. His radical proposals for dealing with mass unemployment by state intervention and deficit financing enjoyed considerable vogue during and after the Second World War. He was also a critic of the punitive peace imposed on Germany after the First World War.

*Road to Wigan Pier* an important book. His strength lay in observation, and no theory was needed to portray the inadequacy of social provision, the decay in urban areas, and the dangers of the coal industry, for which miners received little compensation. He could have acknowledged that his mission, as he wrote in 1931, was *simply to report . . . about the Lower Classes.*[102] He could have put his pen down, viewed what he had done, and left it to others to interpret and debate his findings. To do so, however, would offer up his research to alternative interpretations. So Orwell, always the outsider, turned not upon the 'right', but upon those on the 'left' who might use his material.

Orwell left several hostages to fortune in Part One of *Wigan Pier*. Beyond his experience and documentation were wild fluctuations between specific (but grotesque) portrayals and general platitudes. His affection for the working class was tested by a *half-witted servant girl with huge body, tiny head and rolls of fat at back of neck curiously recalling ham-fat*; by a landlady who, *as usual, does not understand much about politics but has adopted her husband's views as a wife ought to*; by *the astonishing ignorance about and wastefulness of food among the working class people*; and by the abominable Brookers, *chew*[ing] . . .

grievances like a cud, his wife a soft mound of fat and self-pity.[103]

Faith in the masses was restored, however, by Orwell's sweeping tributes to certain groups and images. Coal miners, for example, had the most noble bodies ... with arms and belly muscles of steel. If respect was not on offer, then there was always sympathy for the downtrodden, as in the famous snapshot of a young woman and her dreadful ... destiny ... poking a stick up a foul drain-pipe. If there was a Utopia of the working class, it was a very middle-class affair: When Father, in shirt-sleeves, sits in the rocking chair at one side of the fire reading the racing finals, and Mother sits on the other with her sewing, and the children are happy with a pennorth of mint humbugs, and the dog lolls roasting himself on the rag mat.[104]

Amid the statistics and the prose, The Road to Wigan Pier was a community of sketches clinging to 'reality'. In 1936, Britain was in the middle of a prolonged economic downturn which stemmed not only from the US stock market crash but events closer to home, such as the failure of the gold standard and the subsequent collapse of the Labour government in 1931. More than 20 per cent were unemployed, but the commitment to financial austerity of Labour's successors in the 1930s meant that any social provision was contracting rather than expanding to meet the consequences of the Depression. While a coalition government, led by the Conservatives Stanley Baldwin and then Neville Chamberlain, maintained power, the spectre of 'extreme' movements such as Oswald Mosley's British Union of Fascists and the Communist Party was ever-present. When the royal family was caught up in King Edward VIII's romance with the divorcée Wallis Simpson, leading to his abdication, it appeared that the foundations of British politics and society as well as the economy were breaking down.

Yet at this pivotal time in British history, Orwell made no reference to significant events such as the Jarrow March (1936), in which hundreds of the unemployed marched 300 miles from

Stanley Baldwin (1867–1947) served three times as Conservative Prime Minister: 1923–4, 1924–9 and 1935–7. Dominating the Conservative Party for more than a decade, he succeeded in healing the divisions of previous years. He was credited with taking the country back on to the gold standard, defeating the General Strike, and skilfully handling the abdication crisis. After retiring in 1937, he attracted criticism for his support of appeasement, and for his orthodox economic policies.

Neville Chamberlain (1869–1940) was Conservative Prime Minister from 1937 to 1940. He held a number of posts, including Minister of Health (1924–9) and Chancellor of the Exchequer (1931–7), before succeeding Baldwin as prime minister. Largely outmanoeuvred by Hitler in foreign affairs, Chamberlain reluctantly led the country into war in 1939, but a motion of no confidence the following year after the disastrous Norwegian campaign ended his career.

Oswald Mosley (1896–1980), MP, established the British Union of Fascists in 1932, which stirred up violence against Jews, especially in London's East End. During the Second World War he was imprisoned (1940–3), and he founded the Union Movement in 1948.

north-east England to London to protest against economic conditions, and he gave only a fleeting glimpse of groups like the National Unemployed Workers' Movement (NUWM), despite his recognition that *by far the best work for the unemployed is being done* by the organisation. (He was initially favourable to the NUWM in his diary, as *the lads . . . have been of great service to me,* but he soon turned on it, caricaturing a meeting as *the same sheeplike crowd – gaping girls and shapeless middle-aged women dozing over their knitting – that you see everywhere else.*)[105] With the exception of a diary entry in which Orwell is impressed by slum clearance in Liverpool, he makes no reference to political and economic activity.[106]

So, whatever the power of Orwell's observations, he could not rely on theory, had no broader conception of the British 'situation', and was ambivalent at best about the working class that he supposedly championed. Rather than defend such a position, he went on the offensive in Part Two of the book.

Orwell's answer was a sustained attack on the organised activism of socialists: *Everyone who uses his brain knows that Socialism, as a world-system and wholeheartedly applied, is a way out.* Activists were either *warm-hearted, unthinking* socialists from the working class or a type of middle-class *intellectual, book-trained* socialist *out of touch with common humanity,* with his *soggy half-baked insincerity* and *his pullover, his fuzzy hair, and his Marxian quotation.* These woeful figures were complemented by a *prevalence of cranks,* including *every fruit-juice drinker, nudist, sandal-wearer, sex-maniac, Quaker, 'Nature Cure' quack, pacifist, and feminist in England.* Even the socialist greeting of 'comrade' was suspect, as *that accursed word . . . has kept many a likely recruit away from the Socialist movement.*[107]

The prospect, in Orwell's eyes, was that *the thinking person* is turned away from socialism and that *Fascism may win.*[108] Orwell could offer only a glib solution to this bleak assessment: *Different classes must be persuaded to act together without, for the moment, being asked to drop their class-differences.* Somehow, socialism must capture the *exploited Middle Class.*[109]

This conclusion highlights the legacy of *The Road to Wigan Pier* which was far more destructive than Orwell's immediate call to arms against socialists. The working class was not a potential force to be mobilised; too passive, misguided or ignorant for this, they were a group of people to be fought over in the quest of others for influence and power. Orwell made that very charge against his leftist foes: *This business of class-breaking is a bugger. The trouble is that the socialist bourgeoisie, most of whom give me the creeps, will not be realistic and admit that there are a lot of working-class habits which they don't like and don't want to adopt.*[110]

But Orwell was playing a game of pots and kettles with his statement. Not only had he derided the habits and appearances of various working-class people in some of the most vivid passages in *The Road to Wigan Pier,* but his diary also made clear that they could be no more than pawns in a larger political game. Writing of a meeting led by Oswald Mosley, Orwell concluded: *It struck me how easy it is to bamboozle an uneducated audience.*[111] Far from embracing the working class, Orwell had jettisoned it in favour of the *exploited Middle Class* that must be won over.

Orwell was spoiling for a fight, which continued long after the appearance of *The Road to Wigan Pier*. There could be no acceptance of the 'other' position, no cosy co-existence. The best indication of what was to come was an extraordinary division between Orwell and his publisher, Victor Gollancz.

It was Gollancz who first recognised *Down and Out in Paris and London* as 'an extraordinary and important book',[112] and who had continued to publish Orwell's novels despite disappointing sales. It was Gollancz who had come up with the idea for *The Road to Wigan Pier* and had commissioned Orwell to write it. Most significantly, Gollancz had suggested it be distributed by the Left Book Club, which brought Orwell to a 'mass' audience, even though he utterly disagreed with Orwell's sentiments in Part Two.[113]

However, Gollancz insisted that he be allowed to contribute to the debate with a Foreword to the Left Book Club edition. Some of Gollancz's language has been labelled 'smug' and 'condescending' by Orwell's defenders, such as the note: 'I had, in point of fact, marked well over a hundred minor passages about which I thought I should like to argue with Mr Orwell in this Foreword; but I find now that if I did so the space that I have set aside would be quickly used up, and I should wear out my readers' patience.'[114] Gollancz's main point, however, is an important one: 'It is indeed significant that so far as I can remember (he must forgive me if I am mistaken), Mr Orwell does not once define what he means by Socialism; nor does he explain how the oppressors oppress, nor even what he understands by "liberty" and "justice".'[115]

Orwell was not about to turn his back on such a large readership by withdrawing his book from the Left Book Club. Instead he thanked Gollancz for the Foreword as a discussion *that one always wants.*[116] However, Gollancz had left Orwell in the difficult position of not being able to answer the charge of vagueness, not because the author lacked opportunities to do so but because he lacked the political and economic arguments. Orwell manoeuvred for independence from Gollancz in his correspondence and his future arrangements for publication. As he wrote to his friend Jack Common: *It is rather a good idea to have a foot in both the Gollancz and Secker* [a rival publisher] *camps.*[117]

Still, the battle lines between Orwell and the left were not fixed. The drafting and printing of the book would take almost a year before its appearance in March 1937. Meanwhile Orwell, eager for a quieter life, had rented a small, spartan cottage in a Hertfordshire village in April 1936, and he and Eileen married two months later. In the summer he went to a school, organised by the *Adelphi*, attended by a cross-section of the political left. He gave a talk entitled 'An Outsider Sees the Depressed Areas', participated in the seminars, and debated the tenets of Marxism.

The key test for Orwell, as for so many others on the left, would be Spain, where civil war had broken out when workers took up arms to support the Republican government against an insurgency led by General Franco. As Orwell recalled: *Every anti-Fascist felt a thrill of hope.*[118] By December 1936, days after completing the manuscript of *The Road to Wigan Pier*, he was in Spain, having pawned family silver to pay for the journey. He joined the militia of the Worker's Party of Marxist Unification (POUM), which was supported by Britain's Independent Labour Party.[119] He had enlisted more out of a general desire to help than any well-defined conviction; initially, he had tried to sign up with a communist regiment.

After a week in Barcelona, where he was impressed by the collective spirit of the workers, Orwell was on the battlefront continuously from January to the end of April. Most of the time his unit sat in its dugout waiting for something to happen, but Orwell

On 18 July 1936, General Francisco Franco (1892–1975) staged a military uprising against the Republican government that led to the Spanish Civil War (1936–9). By 1939, with help from Adolf Hitler (1889–1945) and Benito Mussolini (1883–1945), he had defeated the Republicans and become a ruthless dictator. Franco's government – in which the National Movement (incorporating the Spanish fascist party Falange Española) was the only legal party – maintained neutrality throughout the Second World War. Excluded from the United Nations in 1945, Spain's isolation ended in the 1950s

when Franco's anticommunism made him an attractive ally in the Cold War.

distinguished himself by his leadership and bravery. He led infiltrations close to the Fascist lines and, on one occasion, raided an enemy trench.

More exciting action was to come. On leave in Barcelona, he had only a few days with Eileen before the city erupted in fighting among the left. The government, supported by Communist Parties, tried to suppress POUM and the anarchists. Orwell sat on a rooftop guarding POUM's executive building for four days and watched the street fighting. A short-lived truce was arranged, and Orwell returned to his unit, only to be shot in the neck by a sniper.

'Outside Spain, the war looked, at least at first, when all the parties of the Left seemed to be cooperating, the moment of hope for a generation angry at the cynicism, indolence and hypocrisy of an older generation with whom they were out of sympathy.'
HUGH THOMAS[120]

From the end of May to mid-June, he was recovering in a sanatorium outside Barcelona, then travelling to gather the documents for his medical discharge from the militia. During that time, the government resumed its campaign against POUM, banning its newspaper, outlawing the party and arresting members. Orwell returned to Barcelona to find that the police had searched Eileen's hotel room and that his militia commander was in jail. Orwell tried unsuccessfully to obtain the commander's release, then fled to France with Eileen and other associates from the Independent Labour Party (ILP).

A poster from the Spanish Civil War issued by Partido Obrero de Unificacion Marxista (POUM).

Spain did not provoke Orwell's break with the British left, but it consolidated the split. *This Spain business has upset me so that I really can't write about anything else,* he wrote to Jack Common, *and unfortunately what one has to write about is not picturesque stuff but a blasted complicated story of political intrigue between a lot of cosmopolitan Communists, Anarchists etc.*[121] Orwell believed passionately that the left press in Britain, which unconditionally supported the Republican government and denounced organisations like POUM during the events of spring 1937, had sold out the true representatives of the workers. *I honestly doubt,* he wrote angrily, *in spite of all those hecatombs of nuns who have been raped and crucified before the eyes of* Daily Mail *reporters, whether it is the pro-Fascist newspapers that have done the most harm.*[122]

Orwell was further piqued when the leading political journal, the *New Statesman,* rejected an essay on his experiences and observations and then his review of a book on the conflict. His anger was buttressed by Gollancz's rejection of *Homage to Catalonia,* a book of Orwell's recollections and insights, without even a glance at the manuscript. Furious, Orwell did not mince his words, informing friends that *Gollancz is of course part of the Communism-racket.*[123] Even a poem could prompt a furious note. 'Spain 1937' by W H Auden was a rallying cry for supporters of the Republican government:

> What's your proposal? To build the Just City? I will,
> I agree. Or is it the suicide pact, the romantic
> > Death? Very well, I accept, for
> I am your choice, your decision: yes, I am Spain.[124]

The poem is not one of Auden's best (even he later dismissed it as 'trash'). Orwell, however, passed up detailed literary criticism for crude political castigation, lifting the phrase 'necessary murder' out of the poem's context: *Mr Auden's brand of amoralism is only possible if you are the kind of person who is always somewhere else when the trigger is pulled. So much of left-wing thought is a kind of playing with fire by people who don't even know that fire is hot.*[125]

Wystan Hugh Auden (1907–73) was the most influential poet of his generation. Having established his reputation with *Poems* (1930) and *Look Stranger!* (1936), he left Britain for the US in January 1939. *Another Time* (1940) contains some of his most famous poems (such as 'September, 1939' and 'Lullaby'). In later years the politically engaged stance of his youth gave way to more overtly Christian meditations in a dazzling variety of verse forms. In 1956, he was elected Professor of Poetry at Oxford.

Contrary to the later impression that Orwell's views were censored, he was more than able to reach the British public. He did pass up some opportunities: he returned the books the *New Statesman* had sent him to review, and he snapped, when asked in a *Left Review* survey of writers whether he supported the Nationalist or Republican cause: *Will you please stop sending me this bloody rubbish . . . If I did compress what I know and think about the Spanish war into six lines you wouldn't print it.*[126]

Orwell could take such a stand secure in the knowledge that he would be offered far more than six lines to make his case elsewhere. The essay rejected by the *New Statesman*, 'Spilling the Spanish Beans', appeared in the *New English Weekly*, and Orwell reiterated his points in a series of book reviews for a variety of journals. He singled out for praise the work of Franz Borkenau (1900–57), the ex-communist who had been arrested by the Spanish authorities during the Civil War: *The concealment of the main political facts from the public and the maintenance of this deception by means of censorship and terrorism carries with it far-reaching detrimental effects, which will be felt in the future even more than at present.* In contrast, he dismissed the memoirs of an International Brigade member as *tripe.*[127] Most of his reviews served as vehicles for an Orwellian 'history' commemorating POUM and the anarchists[128] and for the author's evolving beliefs. One statement, as much as any sentence Orwell penned after the Second World War, linked his battles abroad and at home: *The test for any pacifist is, does he differ between foreign war and civil war? If he does not, he is simply saying in effect that violence may be used by the rich against the poor but not by the poor against the rich.*[129]

Fredric Warburg agreed to publish *Homage to Catalonia.* At first, the decision seemed rash: only 700 of the first printing of 1,500 copies were sold, and there was no US edition until 1952. Tributes such as the *Observer*'s 'Mr Orwell is a great writer [with his] objective prose of stately, unhurried, unexaggerated clarity' were tucked away on inside pages.[130] Predictably, the *New Statesman* featured V S Pritchett's barb: 'There are many strong arguments for keeping creative writers out of politics and Mr George Orwell is one of them.'[131]

Yet *Homage to Catalonia* established itself, not only because of its quality, but because of a network of eager individuals to promote it for its political as well as

*Homage to Catalonia*

literary merits. Orwell wrote to a friend, Geoffrey Gorer, that the *New Statesman would get a nasty jar when my book on Spain comes out* and that *all the Popular Front stuff that is now being pushed by the Communist press and party, Gollancz and his paid hacks etc etc only boils down to say that they are in favour of British Fascism (prospective) as against German Fascism.* Gorer subsequently noted in *Time and Tide* that 'Homage to Catalonia is [a] phoenix, a book which is at the same time a work of first-class literature and a political document of the greatest importance'. John McNair, who was in Spain and fled it with Orwell, assured readers: 'The writer is not a propagandist. So far as I know, he is a member of no political party.'[132] More tellingly, Herbert Read, the prominent poet, critic and anarchist, wrote to Orwell that the book 'moved me deeply';[133] the praise may have pushed Orwell into openly joining the Independent Labour Party, the same party which had derided his lack of socialist principle in *The Road to Wigan Pier.*

With the passage of time, *Homage to Catalonia* may prove to be Orwell's most influential work.[134] Unlike *The Road to Wigan Pier,* it integrates its observation and polemic. It draws upon the best elements of Orwell's writing style, such as his evocation of atmosphere through sight, sound and smell – *the winter cold, the ragged uniforms of militiamen, the oval Spanish faces, the morse-like tapping of machine-guns, the smells of urine and rotting bread, the tinny taste of bean-stews wolfed hurriedly out of unclean pannikins*[135] – his mix of formal and informal language, and his calculated understatement.

The periodical *Time and Tide: An Independent Non-Party Weekly Review* (1920–77) was originally fiercely left-wing and feminist in its stance, but went through several shades of political opinion before its demise.

*Homage to Catalonia* might also benefit from pre-dating the Cold War. Orwell's last two novels were fought over by right and left in the context of Soviet communism, but *Homage to Catalonia* was largely ignored. With the end of the Cold War, *Animal Farm* and

*Nineteen Eighty-four* start to look rather time-specific or at least tied to the polemics of that ideological contest, but *Homage to Catalonia* is presumed to have 'universal' qualities.

To this day, Orwell has the advantage of the moral high ground. There was no gain, of course, from being a Fascist opponent of the Republican government; however, adherence to an anarchist or Trotskyist challenge, about which little is known outside Spain, could be put forth as a principled stance. From the start, the betrayal of the left is reduced to a Republican government, whose credentials are suspect, against honourable 'workers' whom Orwell will place beyond suspicion: *I recognised it immediately as a state of affairs worth fighting for. Also, I believed that things were as they appeared, that this was really a workers' State and that the entire bourgeoisie had either fled, been killed or voluntarily come over to the workers' side; I did not realise that great numbers of well-to-do bourgeois were simply lying low and disguising themselves as proletarians for the time being.*[136]

Orwell devotes most of the book to his personal experiences. It is an account that uses black humour as a defence against the cold, inactivity and very slow military preparations – *the Spanish are good at many things, but not at making war* – combined with simple praise of the working-class troops as *a sort of temporary working model of the classless society.*[137] Indeed, in the opening pages, Orwell's politics are immersed in a tribute to an Italian volunteer with *the face of a man who would commit murder and throw away his life for a friend . . . Queer, the affection you can feel for a stranger! It was as though his spirit and mine had momentarily succeeded in bridging the gulf of language and tradition in utter intimacy.*[138] A 'decent' left-wing stance, in a far from simple national and international conflict, has become no more complex than the *crystal spirit* of one individual.

Orwell spends two chapters on the politics behind his experiences, but his analysis is limited. He is at his best when he describes the differences between the 'allied' parties in the Republican movement, specifically the hostility of the Spanish government and the Communist Party towards POUM and the Anarchists. However, beyond this perspective, the reader will find no explanation for the outbreak of the civil war, which was not only about 'class' and power for the workers, but also about the place of religion in Spanish life, the optimal type of government, the role of the military, and other divisions within Spain, such as urban versus rural, north versus south, national versus regional. Orwell obscures (and possibly avoids) such complications by always referring to the front-line enemy as 'fascists'; in fact, many of those fighting for the Nationalists had little sympathy for or even knowledge of fascism. Even the title of his book is misleading, for Orwell offers little information about Catalonia, the region centred upon Barcelona which had long sought independence or autonomy within Spain.

By sticking to this limited outline of the conflict, Orwell need never defend himself against alternative interpretations. For example, one argument (put forward by the Republican government and its callow British defenders) was that the rapid fulfilment of anarchist/Trotskyist demands in 1937 would hinder the economic and political arrangements needed for the prosecution of the war against the Nationalists. Another response (put to those who accused the Republicans of being too close to communists and the Soviet Union) was that the situation was fostered by the refusal of other countries such as Britain and France to support the Spanish government.

Orwell's distinctive position, far from being a broad vision of the Civil War or even of the six months that he was in Spain, was not forged until the events of spring 1937. Until then, he was considering service with the International Brigade and writing to Victor Gollancz in a tone which indicated a work of reportage rather than heated commentary: *I shall be going back to the front probably in a few days and barring accidents I expect to be there till about August. After,*

*I think I shall come home as it will be about time I started on another book. I greatly hope I come out of this alive if only to write a book about it. It is not easy here to get hold of any facts outside the circle of one's experience, but with that limitation I have seen a great deal that is of immense interest to me.*[139]

It was only in the turmoil of Barcelona, in which Orwell's service on the front put him in POUM headquarters rather than elsewhere, that he began to make political decisions. He wrote excitedly to Cyril Connolly: *I have seen wonderful things and at last really believe in Socialism which I never did before.*[140] It was this sudden transformation, rather than anti-Orwell vitriol, that has led critics like Raymond Carr to claim that 'Orwell's vision of Spain was blurred by a romanticism that could lapse into political naiveté . . . stunned by the contrast between supposed Spanish simplicity and sincerity and the complex compromises and materialism of life at home.'[141]

Orwell knew he was exaggerating his case. He admitted to a correspondent that he was more sympathetic to POUM in *Homage to Catalonia* than he actually felt: although he found much of interest in the group's political stance, there was *no doubt their way of saying it was tiresome and provocative in the extreme.*[142] To Stephen Spender he apologised that the first two chapters might give the impression that the entire text was *Trotskyist propaganda.*[143]

Orwell's sleight-of-hand can be seen in this simple assertion: *A true history of this war never would or could be written.*[144] While the immediate sentiment was an attack upon the *propaganda* of those backing the Republican government, the underlying argument points to Orwell's pragmatic manoeuvre: he might not have the *truth* about the war, but his integrity and decency would ensure the supremacy of his account and analysis.

The assertion that Orwell is 'right' is a tactic rather than a conclusion, furthered by the extrapolation that, because Orwell is right in this case, he must be right in all cases. Because the British left were naive, misguided or duplicitous in this instance,

SLEIGHT OF HAND

they must always be so. According to Orwell this movement of the deluded or duplicitous consisted of *hack-journalists and the pansy Left, parlour Bolsheviks and sleek little professors.*[145] Orwell was unrelenting in his caricatures of this wrong-headed foe. He had a moment of reflection after his correspondence with Spender: *Funny, I had always used him and the rest of that gang as symbols of the pansy Left, and in fact I don't care for his poems to speak of, but when I met him in person I liked him so much and was sorry for the things I had said about him.*[146]

Orwell would make his own immediate extrapolation, one which led to an extraordinary phase in his political development. The way he saw it, the left had been fighting a deceitful war against fascists in Spain. Now elements of those left-wing groups were forging a Popular Front with the Soviet Union against German fascism, with *the nauseous spectacle of bishops, Communists, cocoa-magnates, publishers, duchesses, and Labour MPs marching arm in arm to the tune of 'Rule Britannia' and all tensing their muscles for a rush to the bomb-proof shelter when and if their policy begins to take effect.*[147] Thus, Orwell, who as late as July 1937 wrote that one *must fight for Socialism and against Fascism,*[148] now saw a greater evil in a left coalition with *a capitalist-Imperialist government: We are one step nearer to the great war 'against Fascism' . . . which will allow fascism, British variety, to be slipped over our necks during the first week.*[149]

Within weeks of the completion of *Homage to Catalonia*, Orwell was placed in a local sanitorium for six months because of a bleeding lesion on his lung. Eileen could afford to visit him only once every two weeks. Yet retreating into isolation was no longer possible: *The impulse of every writer is to 'keep out of politics'. What he wants is to be left alone so that he can go on writing books in peace. But unfortunately it is becoming obvious that this ideal is no more practicable than that of the petty shopkeeper who hopes to preserve his independence in the teeth of the chain-stores.* Orwell concluded: *The time is coming — not next year, perhaps not for ten or twenty years, but it is coming — when every writer will have the choice of being silenced altogether or of producing the dope that a privileged minority demands.*[150]

Orwell joined the Independent Labour Party in June 1938, explaining in the party's weekly journal that *the ILP is the only party which, as a party, is likely to take the right line either against imperialist war or against Fascism when this appears in its British form.*[151] He believed that, rather than defeating fascism and Nazism, the social and economic measures required for the battle with Germany could turn Britain into a fascist state, a position that was in line with his condemnation of the wartime expediency of the Spanish Repub-

Orwell with fellow members of the Independent Labour Party (ILP) contingent to Spain

lican government. He was so concerned about the possible repression that he wrote colleagues of stocking *printing presses etc. in some discreet place* to avoid being silenced.[152] As late as July 1939, he published strident anti-war essays against *Quakers shouting for a bigger army, Communists waving union jacks, Winston Churchill posing as a democrat.*[153]

Orwell had not only embraced pacifism. For the first time he had embraced a philosophy rather than railed against it, and he had done so with a far more developed notion than 'war is bad'. In March 1939, he wrote fellow pacifist Herbert Read: *We are . . . either in for war in the next two years, or for prolonged war-preparation, or possibly only for sham war-preparations designed to cover us other objects, but in any of these cases for a fascising process leading to an authoritarian régime, i.e. some kind of Austro-fascism. So long as the objective, real or pretended, is war against Germany, the greater part of the Left will associate themselves with the fascising process, which will ultimately mean associating themselves with*

THE PACIFIST

*wage-reductions, suppression of free speech, brutalities in the colonies etc.*[154]

The issues occupied his mind even when he turned to fiction. While in the sanatorium, he wrote to Jack Common that he was *keen to get started with my next novel, though . . . I had been thinking what with Hitler, Stalin & the rest of them the day of novel-writing was over. As it is if I start it in August I dare say I'll have to finish it in the concentration camp.*[155] In midsummer 1939, when doctors finally allowed him to resume typing, he returned to the project, entitled *Coming Up for Air*.

In earlier novels, Orwell had referred to his fear of war – as in Gordon Comstock's anticipation of *the reverberations of future wars. Enemy aeroplanes flying over London, the deep threatening hum of the propellers, the shattering thunder of the bombs.* He had written in a book review in November 1936: *The truth is that ours is not an age for mysterious romances about lunatics in ruined chateaux, because it is not an age in which one can be unaware of contemporary reality. You can't ignore Hitler, Mussolini, unemployment, aeroplanes and the radio; you can only pretend to do so, which means lopping off a large chunk of your consciousness. To turn away from everyday life and manipulate black paper silhouettes with the pretence that you are really interested in them, is a sort of game of make-believe, and therefore faintly futile, like telling ghost stories in the dark.*[156]

Now, however, the prospect of war became the central feature of his narrative. His conduit was George 'Fatty' Bowling, an insurance salesman trapped with his wife and children in a dreary suburban existence. George is the physical antithesis of his creator, but when he speaks, it is with Orwell's observations: *The great black bombing plane swayed a little in the air and zoomed ahead so that I couldn't see it . . . In two years' time, one year's time, what shall we be doing when we see one of those things?*[157]

Although *Coming Up for Air* would be another polemic against 1930s British society, two features make George Bowling a more likeable character than Gordon Comstock. The first is his nostalgia for the 'Golden Country' of his youth. The pastoral idyll had appeared in *Keep the Aspidistra Flying* in Gordon's courtship of Rosemary, and it would recur in *Nineteen Eighty-four* and the consummation of Winston's relationship with Julia. In *Coming Up for Air*, however, the 'Golden Country' exists beyond any quest of love and lust; it is the fundamental hope of George's life. It prompts him to strike out one day in search of his childhood village and to give us his autobiography, and his opinions, along the way.

George's story is recounted with a great deal of humour. For the first and only time, Orwell would display a lightness of touch with his character's observations. Thus, what comes out as bitter castigation with Gordon Comstock is George Bowling's rueful shake of the head at the absurdity around him: *Outside the door a newsboy yelled 'Starnoosstannerd!' I saw the poster flapping against his knees: LEGS, FRESH DISCOVERIES. It had got down to that. Two days earlier they'd found a woman's legs in a railway waiting room, done up in a brown-paper parcel, and what with successive editions of the papers, the whole nation was supposed to be so passionately interested in these blasted legs that they didn't need any further introduction. They were the only legs that were news at the moment.*[158]

Even Orwell's previous bark is softened in George's mouth. He finally reaches his childhood watering hole, only to encounter a 1930s version of a hippie. However, whereas Orwell in *The Road to Wigan Pier* had cursed *every fruit-juice drinker, nudist, sandal-wearer, sex-maniac, Quaker, 'Nature Cure' quack, pacifist, and feminist in England*,[159] George's bluster is sad and smile-inducing as he notes those taken up with *vegetarianism, simple life, poetry, nature-worship, roll in the dew before breakfast.* Having softened us up, George then levels his charge: *Say what you like – call it silly, childish, anything – but doesn't it make you puke sometimes to see what they're doing to England, with their bird-baths and their plaster gnomes, and their pixies and tin cans, where the beechwoods used to be?*[160]

Gordon alienates us with the force of his diatribe, but George brings us along, and this is the main political strategy of the novel. The central scene (a forerunner of the Two Minute Hate in *Nineteen Eighty-four*) is a Left Book Club meeting with a guest speaker – *a sort of human barrel-organ shouting propaganda at you* – denouncing fascism. George sees the lecturer as *a mean-looking chap . . . with a bald head which he'd tried rather unsuccessfully to cover up with wisps of hair.* His speech on the Nazis and *Bestial atrocities . . . Hideous outbursts of sadism . . . Rubber truncheons . . . Concentration camps . . . Iniquitous persecution of the Jews* is reduced by Bowling to *What's he doing? Quite deliberately, and quite openly, he's stirring up hatred. Doing the damnedest to make you hate certain foreigners called Fascists.*[161]

Immediately after the Left Book Club meeting, George encounters his old schoolmaster *who stands for Culture.* George is disappointed that he will not discuss Hitler ('*I don't think of him*'), but returns to passages about ancient Greek tyrants. *All the decent people are paralysed,* George concludes. *Dead men and live gorillas. Doesn't seem to be anything between.*[162]

Yet, if the left are wrong in their preparations for conflict with Hitler and other intellectuals are wrong in setting aside the menace, what exactly is to be done? The trip to the 'Golden Country' is no longer a nostalgic excursion, but a quest for a solution through retreat.

But of course there is no going back. George's childhood love is ugly and obese, his fishing pond is gone, and his parents' shop has become a sterile tea-room. Lower Binfield cannot be insulated from what is to come: a bomb from a British wargame hits the High Street. *I'd chucked a pineapple into my dreams,* sighs George, *and lest there should be any mistake the Royal Air Force had followed up with five hundred pounds of TNT.*[163] With no sanctuary, he returns to suburban monotony and his hectoring wife.

For all of his pacifist posturing, when confronted with the difficult questions, Orwell vented some spleen, complained that

American novelist Henry Miller (1891–1980) is best known for *Tropic of Cancer* (1934), *Tropic of Capricorn* (1939), *The Air-Conditioned Nightmare* (1945), and three works – *Sexus* (1949), *Plexus* (1953), and *Nexus* (1960) – known collectively as *The Rosy Crucifixion*. In 1930 he left the US for Europe, and later became something of a spiritual sage for the Beat generation.

things were not what they used to be, and then threw up his hands. The character of George Bowling leads directly to the sentiments of Orwell's essay 'Inside the Whale', in a short collection of the same name published in 1940.

Orwell's ostensible aim was to link Henry Miller's work – which was banned in Britain and the US because of its frank portrayal of sexual relationships – to James Joyce's understanding of the commonplace and Walt Whitman's 'acceptance' of life. This, however, proved to be the starting point for a wholly different project. In 'Inside the Whale' Orwell is concerned, as in *Coming Up for Air*, with the passivity of the ordinary man who *feels himself master of his fate* in his home and local community, but *against major events . . . is as helpless as against the elements.*

Orwell did not condemn this passivity. Indeed, he turned his fire upon the 'political' writers of

American poet Walt Whitman (1819–92) published his most famous collection, *Leaves of Grass*, in 1855; its bold language and themes of political and sexual emancipation causing outrage. His great odes include 'Out of the Cradle Endlessly Rocking' and 'As I Ebb'd with the Ocean of Life', as well as his elegy on Abraham Lincoln, 'When Lilacs Last on the Dooryard Bloom'd'.

the early 1930s such as W H Auden and Stephen Spender. The English communist movement and, by extension, these writers *are mentally subservient to Russia, so their form of Socialism . . . makes mental honesty impossible.* Henry Miller became a positive counterpoint to this viewpoint by being *not only individualistic but completely passive . . . a man who believes the world-process to be outside his control and who in any case hardly wishes to control it.* At a loss for solutions on the eve of the Second World War, Orwell embraced Miller for his resignation, his acceptance that *there was nothing a thinking and sensitive person could do, except to remain human, if possible: Progress and reaction have both turned out to be swindles. Seemingly there is nothing left but quietism – robbing reality of its terrors by simply submitting to it. Get inside the whale – or rather, admit that you are inside the whale ([?] for you are, of course). Give yourself over to the world-process, stop fighting against it or pretending that you control it; simply accept it, endure it, record it. That seems to be the formula that any sensitive novelist is now likely to adopt. A novel on more positive, 'constructive' lines, and not emotionally spurious, is at present very difficult to imagine.*[164]

Where then is the 'political' Orwell that we now celebrate? Salvation, for both the contemporary Orwell and his posthumous reputation, could only come through a diversionary route. If 'Inside the Whale' led to futility (at least for the 'political' Orwell), another essay in the same volume provided a way out.

Orwell had long been interested in Charles Dickens. Dickens offered more than a literary example, given his renown for social observation, but in other ways he was hardly an obvious role model.

Charles Dickens (1812–70) captured the popular imagination as no other novelist had done in works such as *The Pickwick Papers* (1836–7), *Oliver Twist* (1837–8), *Nicholas Nickleby* (1838–9), *The Old Curiosity Shop* (1840–1), *Barnaby Rudge* (1841), *Martin Chuzzlewit* (1843–4), *A Christmas Carol* (1843), *Dombey and Son* (1848), *David Copperfield* (1849–50), *Bleak House* (1852–3), *Hard Times* (1854), *Little Dorrit* (1855–7), *A Tale of Two Cities* (1859), *Great Expectations* (1860–1), and *Our Mutual Friend* (1864–5).

As Orwell stated at the outset of his essay on Dickens, the author of *Oliver Twist* and other classics was neither a proletarian writer nor a revolutionary, since *what is the use of changing the system before you have changed human nature?* Yet, far from being a problem for Orwell, Dickens' vague commitments were ideal for an essayist who seemed to be floundering in the definition of his own mission.

Orwell's task was to convert Dickens from a bourgeois author into *a subversive writer, a radical, one might truthfully say a rebel.* He did this by holding fast to Dickens's *enormous platitude* that *if men would behave decently, the world would be decent* – an acceptable 'radicalism' as opposed to the hard-headed Marxist tradition that Orwell deplored. 'Charles Dickens' thus became a vehicle for Orwell to reduce socialism to a liberalism without theory, a position from which one could *express in a comic, simplified and . . . memorable form the native decency of the common man.*[165]

Orwell concluded by having Dickens view himself in the mirror, although one might suspect that the image the essayist wanted to see was also that of 'George Orwell': *It is the face of a man who is always fighting against something, but who fights in the open and is not frightened, the face of a man who is generously angry – in other words, of a 19th-century liberal, a free intelligence, a type hated with equal hatred by all the smelly little orthodoxies which are now contending for our souls.*

Yet, in the middle of this recasting of himself through the elevation of Dickens, Orwell (inadvertently, one supposes) gave away the shallowness of his own crusade. After years of establishing himself, not as a novelist but as a sharp-eyed moral observer of life around him, Orwell admitted of Dickens (and, thus, of himself): *He has no constructive suggestions, not even a clear grasp of the nature of the society he is attacking, only an emotional perception that something is wrong. All he can finally say is, 'Behave decently,' which . . . is not necessarily so shallow as it sounds.*[166]

# The Rise and Fall of a 'Socialist'

Eight years after his first book, Orwell was still waiting for critical attention. The only comprehensive review of his work had appeared in 1940 by the critic Q D Leavis (1906–81), and even this was brief and decidedly mixed in its assessment. While she praised Orwell's non-fiction, Leavis advised him to give up trying to write novels, commenting that Orwell 'even managed to write a dull novel about a literary man' (*Keep the Aspidistra Flying*). For Orwell to succeed, she concluded, he had to become a uniquely 'political' writer: 'If the revolution here were to happen that he wants and prophesies, the advent of real socialism, he would be the only man of letters we have whom we can imagine surviving the flood undisturbed'.[167]

But what was to be this unique position? Britain's declaration of war on Germany in September 1939 presented Orwell with a difficult choice. A year earlier he had declared: *The first real threat to British interests has turned nine out of ten British Socialists into jingoes;*[168] now he either had to fulfil his declaration of pacifism or undergo a dramatic conversion. For a few months he stalled, concentrating on book reviews and awaiting the publication of *Inside the Whale*, with its uneasy juxtaposition of an attempted abrogation of responsibility and a Dickensian 'liberalism'. He did offer a clue, in a short essay on the Victorian author Charles Reade, that he might be reconsidering his position: [Reade] *was simply a middle-class gentleman with a little more conscience than most . . . offering as complete a detachment from real life as a game of chess or a jigsaw puzzle.*[169]

So, in autumn 1940 Orwell made a belated declaration in the essay 'My Country, Right or Left', published in the collection *Folios of New Writing*. A year earlier, on the eve of the non-aggression pact between Nazi Germany and the Soviet Union, he *dreamed that the war had started.* Apparently the vision absolved him of any previous beliefs regarding aggression, for it showed Orwell *that I was patriotic at heart, would not sabotage or act against my own side, would support the war, would fight in it.*[170] Unable to define his socialist revolution over the previous five years, Orwell now had a suitable alternative: *We are in a strange period of history in which a revolutionary has to be a patriot and a patriot has to be a revolutionary.*[171]

Charles Reade (1814–84) enjoyed great fame as a novelist in his lifetime and was regarded as the natural successor of Dickens. Today he is best remembered for *The Cloister and the Hearth* (1861). His other novels include *Hard Cash* (1863), *Griffith Gaunt* (1866), and *Put Yourself in his Place* (1870).

There remained a problem. Given his strident calls against a war with Germany, how could Orwell justify this sudden shift beyond the rather lame excuse of a portentous dream? The answer came through the elevation not of 'socialism' but of 'Englishness'. *Patriotism of the middle classes is a thing to be made use of,* the new Orwell assured his public. *The people who stand to attention during* God Save the King *would readily transfer their loyalty to a Socialist regime, if they were handled with the minimum of tact* – even if the envisaged revolution seemed a bit of a letdown: *When all is said and done, one's main impression is the immense stolidity of ordinary people, the widespread vague consciousness that things can never be the same again, and yet, together*

Britain declares war on Germany

ENGLISHNESS

*with that, the tendency of life to slip back into the familiar pattern.*[172]

Orwell soon had an opportunity to put his pacifist past behind him and to present an English audience with his vision of the future. In 1941, his friend T R Fyvel began the series of Searchlight Books to *stress Britain's international and imperial responsibilities and the aim of a planned Britain at the head of a greater and freer British Commonwealth, linked with the United States of America and other countries, as a framework of world order.*[173] Orwell wrote one of the first volumes, a short manifesto entitled *The Lion and the Unicorn.*

*The Lion and the Unicorn* contained the clearest statement that Orwell would ever make about his socialism, with a six-point programme for domestic and overseas activity. It included nationalisation of key industries, land and banks, limitations on top incomes, reform of the educational system, and independence for India.

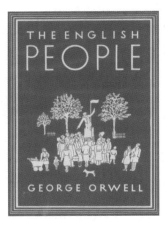

*The English People*, published in 1947, continued Orwell's obsession with the notion of 'Englishness'

He wrote: *From the moment that all productive goods have been declared the property of the State, the common people will feel, as they cannot feel now, that the State is themselves . . . It is all too obvious that our talk of 'defending democracy' is nonsense while it is a mere accident of birth that decides whether a gifted child shall or shall not get the education it deserves.* As for Britain's colonies: *What India needs is the power to work out its own constitution without British interference, but in some kind of partnership that ensures its military protection and technical advice . . . And what applies to India applies, mutatis mutandis, to Burma, Malaya and most of our African possessions.*[174]

This Orwellian programme, however, was situated within a socialism that would *not be doctrinaire, nor even logical.*[176] Five years after *The Road to Wigan Pier*, Orwell was still unable or unwilling to provide a systematic analysis of his position. He certainly was not

*In practice, the majority of Indians* are infe-*rior to Europeans and one can't help feeling this and, after a little while, act accordingly.* GEORGE ORWELL, April 1942 [175]

going to link it to the platform of any political party or organisation. Instead, he went over the heads of the politicians, the bureaucrats, and the intellectuals to appeal to the 'common man'.

He did so with an 'England' which owed little to observation and much to myth and cliché; a country of *solid breakfasts and gloomy Sundays, smoky towns and winding roads, green fields and red pillar-boxes . . . a land where the bus conductors are good-tempered and the policemen carry no revolvers.*[177] He assured his readers: *Above all, [England]* is *your civilization, it is you. However much you hate it or laugh at it, you will never be happy away from it for any length of time. The suet puddings and the red pillar-boxes have entered into your soul. Good or evil, it is yours, you belong to it, and this side of the grave you will never get away from the marks that it has given you.*[178]

Orwell could only provide the wonders of this 'Englishness' with some twisting and turning in his socialist politics. He noted a *decay of ability in the ruling class* but, to hold his England together, added that they were *morally fairly sound.* Their faults lay in aptitude rather than malice: *What is to be expected of them is not treachery, or physical cowardice, but stupidity, unconscious sabotage, an infallible instinct for doing the wrong thing.*[179] So the author of *The Road to Wigan Pier* could blithely assure the reader that *patriotism is usually stronger than class-hatred.* The inept ruling elite would just melt away before an epiphany (culminating in the British retreat at Dunkirk), in which *the working class, the middle class and even a section of the business community could see the utter rottenness of private capitalism.*[180]

Unlike *The Road to Wigan Pier*, which had ended with no idea of the way forward, and *Homage to Catalonia*, which substituted a paean to the *crystal spirit* for lack of any prospects after the battle of

Barcelona, *The Lion and the Unicorn* staked a claim in the debate over the future of the country. It did so with some success: the *Times Literary Supplement* found in Orwell's 'brilliant essay an eager desire to bridge the gulf between the too long silent strength of British patriotism and the unrooted, internationalist left-wing ideas which have dominated British thought between the wars'.[181]

The challenge for Orwell was that he would be a lone leader of the march into England's promised land. It could not be otherwise, for he could not trust anyone else on the left. In 'My Country, Right or Left' he pointed to those whom he considered suspect: *It is exactly the people whose hearts have never leapt at the sight of a Union Jack who will flinch from revolution when the time comes.*[183] *The Lion and the Unicorn* continued in this vein, as Orwell sneered at those who *take their cookery from Paris and their opinions from Moscow*; adding that *England is perhaps the only great country whose intellectuals are ashamed of their own nationality.*[184] In contrast, Orwell could be trusted because of his decency: *It is curious that I always attribute these devious motives to other people, being anything but cunning myself and finding it hard to use indirect methods even when I see the need for them.*[185]

> *Wherever one looks, one sees that any real struggle means revolution. Churchill evidently can't see or won't accept this, so he will have to go.* GEORGE ORWELL, June 1940[182]

The German–Soviet Non-Aggression Pact of 1939 had expanded the range of Orwell's surveillance (and, indeed, may have been the catalyst for his abrupt transformation from pacifist to patriot warmonger). According to Orwell, before the pact was signed, the socialists were turning decent people towards fascism; after the event, the socialists and the pacifists (embodied in the *quisling*

Stalin and von Ribbentrop in 1939

*intellectual*)[186] gave shelter to a fascist-communist axis: *Germany is going Bolshevik because of Hitler and not in spite of him.*[187]

Orwell, the armchair general, promised his readers that the revolution would not be a bloody one (that was the European way) and that, amid the turmoil caused by the war and economic sacrifices at home, the common people would assert their moral values so forcefully that they would emerge as the new English/British regime. *Like all else in England,* [the revolution] *happens in a sleepy, unwilling way, but it is happening,* Orwell assured his readers. *The right men will be there when the people really want them, for it is movements that make leaders and not leaders movements.*[189]

> *No doubt a strong pro-Nazi party exists in Russia, and I dare say Stalin is at the head of it . . . If the Soviet regime is simply wiped out and Stalin killed or taken prisoner, many Communists would in my opinion transfer their loyalty to Hitler.*
> GEORGE ORWELL, June 1941[188]

Such assertions are rather vague. They had to be, for Orwell had no clear idea of his potential troops. He was both insecure and inconsistent in describing his would-be followers. Just after the start of the war, Orwell speculated to Victor Gollancz (with whom there seems to have been an accommodation, if not a reconciliation): *Perhaps when the pinch comes the common people will turn out to be more intelligent than the clever ones.*[190] By October 1940, his hopes were dimmed by the prospect that the working class were *more frightened than the middle class;*[191] however, six months later he was claiming that the intellectual limitations of the working class would prove its salvation: *You have all the time the sensation of kicking against an impenetrable wall of stupidity. But of course at times their stupidity has stood them in good stead. Any European nation situated as we are would have been squealing for peace long ago.*[192]

> *As to the great proletarian novel, I really don't see how it's to come into existence . . . The thing is that all of us talk & write two different languages, & when a man from, say, Scotland or even Yorkshire writes in standard English he's writing something quite as different from his own tongue as Spanish is from Italian. I think the first real prole novel that comes along will be spoken over the radio.*
> GEORGE ORWELL, April 1938[193]

Thus, even as he was setting out his revolutionary vision, Orwell was floundering. He complained to a friend about his inability to serve in the military because of his weak lungs: *I have so far completely failed to serve* [His Majesty's] *government in any capacity, though I want to, because it seems to me that now we are in this bloody war we have got to warn it and I would like to lend a hand.*[194] Training in the Home Guard, he could only write to journals with plans that bordered on the fantastic. ARM THE PEOPLE, he proclaimed, demanding that hand grenades and shotguns be given to Guard units that would become *a democratic guerrilla force*. (Unsurprisingly, the government was unwilling to distribute hand grenades and shotguns to potential revolutionaries.)[195]

Orwell in the Home Guard, *c.*1940–3

Orwell's march towards revolution was aborted by an ill-advised, if patriotic, career move. At the start of the war, Eileen had joined the Censorship Department of the Ministry of Information, and after several months Orwell reluctantly moved back to London to be with her. Back in London, however, he was doing little more than writing a weekly column on film and theatre for *Time and Tide*. The reviews were undistinguished – even Orwell's admirers have labelled them 'hasty, heavy-handed, and banal'[196] – save for a critique of Charlie Chaplin's *The Great Dictator* (1940), which hailed the film's decency even if it did not appeal to dubious intellectuals and *sleek professors*.[197] So in autumn 1941, Orwell accepted a temporary contract from the Empire Department of the British Broadcasting Corporation (BBC), attending an intensive course for would-be producers of radio programs. He was put in charge of cultural programming for India and south-east Asia.

For two years his main role was to book guests to appear on the BBC. T S Eliot, Stephen Spender and the Welsh poet Dylan Thomas

Orwell joined the Empire Department of the BBC, in charge of cultural programming for India and south-east Asia

(1914–53) read their poems; novelist E M Forster (1879–1970) gave talks on his writing. Other broadcasts evaluated politics, history, science and customs, all to project overseas the virtues of a 'British' – and, more specifically, an 'English' – way of life. Orwell also wrote news commentaries, but none of these had more than a passing impact. 'From a studio deep under Oxford Street,' recalled Malcolm Muggeridge, Orwell 'beamed at listeners in Cawnpore, Kuala Lumpur and Rangoon – assuming, of course, that there were any – 'Areopagitica', 'The Waste Land' read by the author in person, and other gems of western culture, with a view to enthusing them for the Allied cause. When I delicately suggested that this may well have failed to hit its target, the absurdity of the enterprise struck him anew, and he began to chuckle, deep

'Areopagitica' (1644) was a defence of the freedom of the Press by poet and republican John Milton (1604–74), author of *Paradise Lost* (1667).

T S Eliot's 'The Waste Land' (1922) is regarded by many as the greatest poem of the 20th century and the high point of modernism. The poet himself claimed it was 'just a piece of rhythmical grumbling'.

in his throat, very characteristic of him and very endearing.'[198]

Less than a year after taking the job, Orwell reflected that the futile BBC broadcasts – *just shot into the stratosphere*[199] – were distracting him from more important tasks. This, however, was a convenient excuse for a campaign which was always going to be a non-starter. By 1941, Orwell had alienated entire sections of British political and intellectual life. The right, of course, were unlikely to join his crusade, but socialists, anarchists, pacifists, Labour Party activists, *pansy poets*, and journals such as the *New Statesman* had no cause to trust a writer who, with a sudden change of heart, could move from alliance to condemnation. The pacifist George Woodcock, who later became a friend and admiring critic of Orwell, made this damning charge in the *Partisan Review* in 1942: 'If we are to expose antecedents, Orwell does not come off very well. Comrade Orwell, the former police officer of British imperialism (from which the fascists learnt all they know) in those regions of the Far East where the sun at last sets for ever on the bedraggled Union Jack! Comrade Orwell, former fellow-traveller of the pacifists and regular contributor to the pacifist *Adelphi* – which he now attacks! Comrade Orwell, former extreme left-winger, ILP partisan and defender of anarchists (see *Homage to Catalonia*)! And now Comrade Orwell who returns to his old imperialist allegiances and works at the BBC conducting British propaganda to fox [i.e., mislead] the Indian masses!'[200]

Far from seeking to mend relations and forge alliances, Orwell retorted: *Pacifism is objectively pro-Fascist. This is clear common sense . . . I am not interested in pacifism as a moral phenomenon.* He offered to differentiate between individuals in his judgement *of true intellectuals* (although he provided no examples), as he continued to target *the Catholic gang, the Stalinist gang, and the present pacifist or, as they are sometimes nicknamed, the Fascifist gang.* (As for his past, Orwell offered a response to the charge that he served imperialism in Burma and at the BBC; however, he renounced the POUM that he had praised in *Homage to Catalonia* and, somehow, failed to mention his own pacifist proclamations of 1937–9.)

The most impressive, or distressing, feature of Orwell's reply was his ability to combine his portrayal of pacifists as accomplices of National Socialism with a denunciation of others who might have been 'anti-imperial' allies, even as Orwell implicitly admitted that he would never subject his arguments to the rigours of 'theory': *As an ex-Indian civil servant, it always makes me shout with laughter to hear, for instance, Gandhi named as an example of the success of non-violence. As long as 20 years ago, it was cynically admitted in Anglo-Indian circles that Gandhi was very useful to the British Government. So he will be the Japanese if they get there. Despotic governments can stand 'moral force' till the cows come home; what they fear is physical force. But though not much interested in the theory of pacifism, I am interested in the psychological process by which pacifists who have started out with an alleged horror of violence end up with a marked tendency to be fascinated by the success and power of Nazism.*[201]

Orwell, on his own, could not succeed in his revolution. In mid-1942 he was still predicting a political crisis as people were *fed up and ready for a radical policy*. Yet he also assessed that, while this meant more social equality, it did not mean socialism – and his own revolution concluded with thoughts of *crocuses in the park, another day pear blossom, another day hawthorn.*[202] Orwell's uncertainties also mounted up in private. He recorded in his diary his *feeling of frustration, the impossibility of getting anything done, even any successful piece of scoundrelism,*[203] while in a curious compromise, if not recantation, he was acknowledging to Woodcock and others that he had been *rather rude* to them in the *Partisan Review*. He then proceeded to rubbish the BBC: *For heaven's sake don't think I don't see how they are using me . . . God knows I have the best means of judging what a mixture of whore-shop and lunatic asylum it is for the most part.*[204] To another friend he added, *I'm just an orange that's been trodden upon by a very dirty boot.*[205]

Orwell's growing uncertainty suddenly turned into pessimism in early 1943 and he grumbled that *The forces of reaction have won hands down.* His dislike of a capitalist future overrode even his belief in an Anglo-American alliance as he wrote of *the dreary world which the American millionaires and their British hangers-on intend to impose upon us.*[206] Of course, the fault lay with the socialists, although Orwell was not sure where exactly to place the blame. Sometimes his fellow intellectuals had been mistreated: *There is no knowing just how much the Socialist movement has lost by alienating the literary intelligentsia, but it has alienated them, partly by confusing tracts with literature, and partly by having no room in it for a humanistic culture.*[207] Sometimes they were the source of the problem: *In the last 20 years Western civilisation has given the intellectual security without responsibility . . . He has been in the position of a young man living on an allowance from a father whom he hates. The result is a deep feeling of guilt and resentment, not combined with any genuine desire to escape.*[208] The specifics did not matter because, by the end of 1944, Orwell had given up: *There has been no real shift of power and no increase in genuine democracy. The same people still own the property and usurp all the best jobs.*[209]

When he resigned from the BBC in September 1943, Orwell's output was limited to anonymous fortnightly commentaries for the *Observer* and a weekly book review for the *Manchester Evening News.* His sharpest writing was being read not in Britain but in the US through his 'London Letters' for the *Partisan Review.* It had been two-and-a-half years since he had published a short book, four since he had completed a novel, almost six since he had written a documentary.

Then another benefactor appeared. In the early 1930s it was Sir Richard Rees; in 1936 it was Victor Gollancz; now it was the Labour

A brilliant speaker, the Labour politician Aneurin 'Nye' Bevan (1897–1960) clashed with the Labour Party in 1939 over its complacent attitude towards Hitler. He edited the socialist newspaper *Tribune* (1940–5) and, as Minister of Health (1945–51) launched the National Health Service in 1948.

Party and Aneurin 'Nye' Bevan. The war had revived Labour, split and decimated in the 1930s. With the collapse of the Chamberlain cabinet in the adversity of 1940, a coalition government including Labour representatives had to be formed to hold the country together. *Tribune*, as the publication associated with the left of the party, gained in prominence and influence.

Bevan, the Labour MP who was the driving force behind *Tribune*, was considered by many as a 'maverick'. He had advocated confrontation with Germany when most were still calling in 1938 for an avoidance of war, and he was briefly expelled from the Labour Party for demanding a coalition of European socialist parties. It could be surmised, then, that Bevan saw in Orwell a forceful but independent writer who could put forth provocative opinions in wartime. He told the other members of the *Tribune* board: 'George has alighted on our desk, as he'll be when he leaves, free as a bird. We'll be glad when he's with us. We'll accept the fact that there will be times when he will fly off.'[210]

Orwell was far from an ideal editor, lacking both the time and the organisational skills. Piles of manuscripts, some of which would be reviewed, others never read, filled the office, and he commissioned more articles than he could ever use. He compensated for this, however, with his weekly column, 'As I Please'. The format was perfect for Orwell. With the freedom to consider any subject, Orwell could blend literary, cultural and political commentary

The origins of the Labour Party lie in the trades-union movement of the 19th century. In 1922, Labour became one of the two major political parties in Britain and formed a government (1924, 1929–31, 1931–5) under Ramsay MacDonald (1866–1937). The party won a huge majority in 1945 under Clement Attlee (1883–1967), enabling it to introduce far-reaching reforms, including nationalisation and a comprehensive social security system.

'Aneurin Bevan, I believe, did more than any other man of his time to keep alive democratic socialism as the most adventurous, ambitious, intelligent, civilised and truly liberal of modern doctrines.'
MICHAEL FOOT[211]

NATIONAL UNION OF
JOURNALISTS
7 John Street, Bedford Row, London, W.C.1
'Phone :                         Telegrams :
HOLborn 2258              Natujay Holb, London
This is to certify that
Mr. GEORGE ORWELL
of The Tribune

is a member of the T - & P.
Branch of the National Union of Journalists.
Leslie R. Alfonso  Branch Sec.
(Address) 66, Priory Gdns., N.6.
Member's Sig.

Orwell's NUJ card

by writing about his eclectic interests. Because the columns were short, usually no more than several hundred words, the lack of depth and resolution that hindered Orwell's lengthy essays and books was not exposed. T R Fyvel, Orwell's successor as literary editor, later paid him tribute, saying that Orwell's 'As I Please' column 'gave the same distinction to the paper's literary end that Bevan's socialist line gave to the front half. It was written in that style of personal reportage which had produced some of the most vivid literature of the period, the style of a writer turned reporter who has participated in the events he describes and so given them an extra dimension – Hemingway at Caporetto and in the Caribbean, Orwell in Burma and Barcelona, Isherwood in Berlin, Koestler in jail, Vincent Sheean in various places. This literary style, particular to its age, can probably not be repeated (Norman Mailer describing a march on the Pentagon is, by comparison, writing a deliberately mannered account about a "Happening").'[212]

Orwell's first column illustrated the range of his commentary with items on the behaviour of American soldiers, his pamphlet collection, and the work of the 19th-century English author Mark Rutherford. With this diversity of interests, 'As I Please' was far more than a political pulpit for Orwell. Indeed, it was more effective in establishing him as an English cultural icon.

In 1940, in an essay on 'Boys' Weeklies' (included in *Inside the Whale*), Orwell had opened up the realm of 'popular culture' to serious scrutiny. By evaluating the style and content of these comics, he was able to observe their moral code: a clear distinction between 'good' and 'bad' boys; no mention of sex or religion; and distaste for (but also a fascination with) drinking, smoking and gambling. Orwell went further, however, with some sharp comments on class, notably the *perfectly deliberate incitement to wealth-fantasy,* with the glamour of public school life, and the entry of the working class only *as comics or semi-villains.* He placed the politics of the weeklies as pre-1914 Conservative and noted their assumption that *foreigners are funny.* While newer versions of the comics emphasised scientific and futuristic themes and the emergence of *bully-worship and the cult of violence,* Orwell contended that the weeklies of the 1940s were stuck in a timewarp, still committed to class prejudices and *sodden in the worst illusions of 1910.*[213]

'Mark Rutherford' was the pseudonym of William Hale White (1831–1913). A civil servant, he wrote literary journalism and is best known for *The Autobiography of Mark Rutherford, Dissenting Minister* (1881), a powerful account of one man's loss of faith.

In the war years, Orwell would take up the unique position of interpreting exalting, and defining 'popular' culture as scholarly and propagandist. He could publish a provocative critique of the English seaside postcard – with its *very 'low' humour* and women *monstrously parodied, with bottoms like Hottentots* – symbolising a battle between *noble folly and base wisdom,* and still conclude in praise of Englishness: *The corner of the human heart that* [these postcards] *speak for might easily manifest itself in worse forms, and I for one should be sorry to see them vanish.*[214] He could attack the very un-English surrealist painter Salvador Dali (1904–89) for *diseased and disgusting pictures* – a *direct, unmistakable assault on sanity and decency; and even . . . on life itself,* only to better define the difference between art and morality: *One ought to be able to hold in one's head simultaneously the two facts that Dali is a good draughtsman and a disgusting human being. The one does not invalidate or, in a sense, affect the other.*[215]

Orwell could even use crime fiction to hold up English decency above a cruder American version, comparing the Raffles stories of E W Hornung, popular in Britain about 1900, with the US-influenced novel *No Orchids for Miss Blandish* by James Hadley Chase. Raffles might be a burglar, but he is a *gentleman* burglar, and

Ernest William Hornung (1866–1921) was the creator of Raffles, the gentleman burglar, public-school man and cricketer, who first appeared in *The Amateur Cracksman* (1899).

whatever standards he has *are not to be violated.* He will not commit murder, he avoids violence where possible, he is chivalrous with women, and *above all, he is intensely patriotic.* In contrast, *No Orchids for Miss Blandish* was *a header into the cesspool* with *eight full-dress murders* and other casual killings, flogging and torture of women, and even *a strip-tease act.* In changing times, Orwell could even find something to like about the English class system given the *great numbers of English people who are partly Americanised in language and, one ought to add, in moral outlook ... One is driven to feel that snobbishness, like hypocrisy, is a check upon behaviour whose value from a social point of view has been underrated.*[216]

Orwell had broken through by introducing 'high-brow' journals

'James Hadley Chase' was the pseudonym of English novelist René Raymond (1906–85) whose stories are almost always set in the US. He adopted the manner of the American 'hard-boiled' school and had an immediate success with *No Orchids for Miss Blandish* (1939).

to popular culture, but the importance of 'As I Please' and his other newspaper contributions was that Orwell's definition of 'Englishness' would reach a wider audience. In the *Evening Standard* he published a series of paeans to English cuisine,

extolling the virtues of *kippers, Yorkshire pudding, Devonshire cream, muffins and crumpets,* the perfect cup of tea and the ideal pub. In the *Manchester Evening News* he reviewed a book on cricket only to conclude that, although the game was dull, it was *a useful reminder that peace means something more than a temporary stoppage of the guns.*[217] 'Culture' had become a defence against the trials of modern politics. In a tribute to the *common toad* emerging from hibernation he could somehow conclude: *The atomic bombs are piling up in the factories,* the police are prowling through the cities, the lies are streaming from the loudspeakers, but the earth is still going around the sun, and neither the dictators nor the bureaucrats, deeply as they disapprove of the process, are able to prevent it.[218]

Orwell's reinvention of himself as a cultural commentator is even more striking when contrasted with the halting development of his politics. In an early column he tried to defend socialism by distinguishing it from the illusions of Utopianism: *Socialists don't claim to be able to make the world perfect; they claim to be able to make it better.*[220] He made barbed remarks about the continued division of property among a few thousand families who were *just about as useful as so many tapeworms*, as well as on the trap of poverty: *Our society is not only so arranged that if you have money you can buy luxuries with it . . . It is also so arranged that if you don't have money you pay for it at every hour of the day with petty humiliations and totally unnecessary discomforts.*[221] There was, however, no advance on his observations of the 1930s, no detailed consideration of a way forward.[222] A typical Orwell essay always ends in contradictory bluster: *This business about the moral superiority of the poor is one of the deadliest forms of escapism the ruling class has evolved*, for instance, in which he momentarily forgets his own moral elevation of the working class in *The Road to Wigan Pier*.[223]

*If you look up 'tea' in the first cookery book that comes to hand you will probably find that it is unmentioned; or at most you will find a few lines of sketchy instructions which give no ruling on several of the most important points. This is curious, not only because tea is one of the mainstays of civilisation in this country, as well as in Eire, Australia and New Zealand, but because the best manner of making it is the subject of violent disputes.*
GEORGE ORWELL, January 1946[219]

The legacy of 'As I Please' was not a systematic affirmation of the 'decent' political man, but individual observations that would later take on a greater significance for Orwell. His column introduced the idea of super-states (which he would develop in *Nineteen Eighty-four*), based on the analysis of the American political philosopher James Burnham (1905–87): *Not only will each of them be too big to be* conquered, but they will be under no necessity to trade with one another, and in a position to prevent all contact between their nationals.[224] There was a strange intervention on the Jewish question, with Orwell contending that it was no use talking about the persecution of the Jews in Germany because the neurosis lies very deep, and just what it is that people hate when they say that they hate a non-existent entity called the 'Jews' is still uncertain.[225] And he also made the observation (pertinent in the light of his later connection with the British secret services): The important thing is to discover which individuals are honest and which are not; the usual blanket accusation merely makes this more difficult.[226]

At last, Orwell had the assurance of a large readership for his wisdom, but his revolutionary vision was more illusory than ever. Englishness was proving to be little more than a bulwark against the whisky-swilling Scottish drunks who administered the empire, the agitators under the delusion that Eire, Scotland, or even Wales could preserve its independence unaided and owes nothing to British protection, and the small but violent separatist movements which exist within our own island.[228]

One of the few complex and incisive exceptions to Orwell's muddled political conceptions in 'As I Please' was an item on the treatment of French female 'collaborators'. Noting a newspaper photograph of the women, heads shaved and swastikas branded on their faces, led through the streets of Paris, Orwell remembered the Jews who were marched past the German public. He quoted Nietzsche, 'He who fights too long against dragons becomes a dragon himself, and if you gaze too long into the abyss, the abyss will gaze into you.'[227]

In 1944, Orwell tried once more to rally the troops: By the end of another decade it will be finally clear whether England is to survive as a great nation or not. And if the answer is to be 'Yes', it is the common people who must make it so.[229] At the same time, he was retreating into depression: The bourgeoisie are coming more and more out of their holes; the Labour Party has sunk a few feet deeper in everyone's estimation; the intelligentsia were caught up in extraordinary contradictions or astonishing servility to the Soviet Union; and pacifists were notable for

Thousands stream to the Central Hall, Westminster in London to celebrate Labour's election victory

their *sheer cowardice.*[230] As victory neared in 1945, Orwell snapped at his old enemies: *Particularly on the Left, political thought is a sort of masturbation fantasy in which the world of facts hardly matters.*[231]

The paucity of Orwell's socialism was illustrated by the unexpected triumph of the Labour Party in the 1945 general election. Not only did Labour win a secure parliamentary majority for the first time, but it did so with a commitment to the institution and development of a welfare state. Orwell had spectacularly failed to foresee Labour's landslide victory. As early as January 1944 he had dismissed the party's future: *In practice the existing Labour leaders, who are terrified of power, will certainly keep on the Coalition and demand very little in return, unless very strongly prodded from below: in which case we shall get a Parliament similar to the present one but with a stronger Opposition.*[232] Six months later, he did not believe Labour would *make a serious effort to win* the general election.[233] In June 1945, a few weeks before polling, he did concede that it was *conceivable that*

*Labour* [might] *win the election against the will of its leaders,* but he was preoccupied with *the lack of reaction of any kind by the British people.*[234]

There were occasional glimpses of a more perceptive and positive Orwell. He was no fan of the new Prime Minister Clement Attlee (who reminded him of *a recently dead fish, before it has had time to stiffen*), but he paid fulsome tribute to Aneurin Bevan, the director of *Tribune*, who had unexpectedly become Minister of Health. *More of an extremist and more of an internationalist* than Labour colleagues, Bevan thought and felt *as a working man,* though he had *no sign of ordinary class consciousness.*[235]

In his 'Letter from London' of autumn 1945, Orwell finally admitted he was *wrong in suggesting that the Labour leaders might flinch from power.* Ultimately, however, he saw Labour's ascendancy as no more than a minor rearrangement of the political furniture: *One cannot take this slide to the Left as meaning that Britain is on the verge of revolution . . . The mood of the country seems to me less revolutionary, less Utopian, even less helpful than it was in 1940 or 1942.* Lost in his pessimism, Orwell put up his hands once more: *Heaven knows whether his Government has any serious intention of introducing Socialism, but if it has, I don't see what there is to stop it.*[236]

For Orwell, there was no longer a revolution, no programme of action, no fundamental economic or social principle. Even any enthusiasm for Labour had 'cooled perceptibly and rapidly', according to George Woodcock, now Orwell's friend.[237] Yet, as with his essay on Charles Dickens, Orwell carefully left himself a political role. Ever vigilant against foes, especially on the left, he would be the valiant sentinel warning his readers away from propaganda.

Orwell's concern with the lies of intellectuals, the press and politicians had been fostered by his experiences in Spain, and had emerged before the Second World War. He had even anticipated a famous scene in *Nineteen Eighty-four* when he claimed in January 1939: *It is quite possible that we are descending into an age in which 2+2 will* make 5 when the Leader says so.[238] The theme of the intertwined nature of art, language and propaganda was refined in essays such as 'New Words' – *The art of writing is in fact largely the perversion of words, and I would even say that the less obvious this perversion is, the more thoroughly it has been done*[239] – and in Orwell's radio broadcasts: *Whoever feels the value of literature, whoever sees the central part it plays in the development of human history, must also see the life and death necessity of resisting totalitarianism, whether it is imposed on us from without or from within.*[240]

However, Orwell's direct assault on the language of the enemy only began in earnest in 1943. Before then, Orwell the BBC employee had wavered. *This is the most truthful war that has been fought in modern times,* he said, seeing the necessity for British propaganda: *All propaganda is lies, even when one is telling the truth. I don't think this matters so long as one knows what one is doing, and why.*[241]

Once again he sought clarity in his writing by focussing on his left-wing foes. In 'Literature and the Left' (published in *Tribune*), Orwell proposed to separate good writing, as well as humanity, from the threat of a poet like W H Auden, who was *watching his navel in America.*[242] In an essay on the Hungarian-born British author Arthur Koestler (1905–83) he put forward the proposition that *England is lacking . . . in what one might call concentration-camp literature. The special world created by secret-police forces, censorship of opinion, torture and frame-up trials is, of course, known about and to some extent disapproved of, but it has made very little emotional impact. One result of this is that there exists in England almost no literature of disillusionment about the Soviet Union.'*[243]

Orwell used 'As I Please' to define 'history' and propaganda,[244] but ultimately he returned to the basic notion of language. *For quite long periods,* he claimed, *people can remain undisturbed by obvious lies, either because they simply forget what is said from day to day or because they are under such a constant propaganda bombardment that they become anaesthetised to the whole business.*[245] The 'perversion' might be practised by countries such as Nazi Germany, but Orwell kept his gaze fixed on the left. *Marxist English*, he noted, was *a style of writing that bears the same relation to writing real English as doing a jigsaw puzzle bears to painting a picture.*[246]

It seemed that Orwell had little 'truth' to offer beyond his vigilance and good character: *In the last analysis, our only claim to victory is that if we win the war we shall tell fewer lies about it than our adversaries.*[247] Yet he had established the authority that would carry his reputation to his death and far beyond: in a world where *the artist must have some kind of patron – a ruling class, the Church, the State, or a political party,*[248] Orwell alone could be trusted. *All the appeasers, e.g., Professor E H Carr, have switched their allegiance from Hitler to Stalin* – and as for intellectuals, they were *more totalitarian in outlook than the common people.*[249]

Moreover, Orwell now had the time and resources to be an effective guardian. While he had to fulfil his editorial duties, he was not under the kind of pressure he had experienced in the 1930s, which both fuelled and hampered his literary output. Finally, he could pursue another novel, and set to work developing an idea which had occurred to him six years before: *On my return from Spain*, he explained, *I thought of exposing the Soviet myth in a story that could be easily understood by almost anyone and which could be easily translated into other languages. However the actual details of the story did not come to me for some time until one day . . . I saw a little boy, perhaps ten years old, driving a huge cart-horse along a narrow path, whipping it whenever it tried to turn. It struck me that if only such animals became aware of their strength we should have no power over them, and that men exploit animals in much the same way as the rich exploit the proletariat.*[250]

The world was about to learn of the ultimate 'revolution betrayed', the failure of the left that would be known as *Animal Farm*.

# The Liberal's Legacy

In February 1944, Orwell wrote to Gleb Struve, a fellow critic of Soviet communism: *I am writing a little squib which might amuse you when it comes out, but it is so not OK politically that I don't feel certain in advance that anyone will publish it.*[251] Britain and the Soviet Union were wartime allies in the fight against Germany, but that only spurred Orwell's belief that readers should be reminded of the perils of a revolution which ended by oppressing workers rather than ensuring their freedom and rights. This would be the first book in which he *tried, with full consciousness of what I was doing, to fuse political purpose and artistic purpose into one whole.*[252]

The draft was finished within four months. Orwell was aware of the potential for political controversy of his *little fairy story.* He first showed the manuscript to Victor Gollancz, to whom he was still under contract for his next novel, to ensure Gollancz's rejection, since he *could not possibly publish a general attack*[253] on the Soviet Union during the war. Then Orwell's travails began. Readers from Jonathan Cape, the next publisher he approached, recommended publication, but an official in the Ministry of Information pressed the firm to retract its

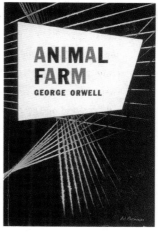

The 1946 jacket for *Animal Farm*

decision.[254] (It has since been alleged that the official, Peter Smollett, was a Soviet agent.) T S Eliot, who had turned down *Down and Out in Paris and London*, now earned the distinction of rejecting Orwell twice. Eliot complained that the draft lacked 'a positive point of view' and wilfully misread it as an argument for 'more communism'.[255] In the US, the Dial Press, showing no appreciation for satire, observed that 'it was impossible to sell animal stories in the USA'.[256] Orwell finally accepted a contract with Fredric Warburg, whose firm was gaining a reputation for publishing books from a left viewpoint that had been turned down elsewhere.

The difficult publication history of *Animal Farm* has raised the issue of whether Orwell's position on censorship was shaped by his experience of being himself 'censored'. But Gollancz did not turn down the manuscript through any affinity for Soviet communism (in 1941, Gollancz had published *The Betrayal of the Left*, to which Orwell contributed), but because the Soviets were now allied with Britain in the war against Germany. Other publishers turned it down for the same reason. The barriers to *Animal Farm*'s publication were not so much the result of government censorship as a wartime environment in which Britain's allies were treated kindly.

When it did finally appear, *Animal Farm* was slow to make an impression. Warburg was a relatively small publisher and had limited supplies of paper under wartime rationing, so the book was not published until August 1945. The first print run of 4,500 copies sold out in weeks, but a second run of 10,000 could not be produced until November. Moreover, several US publishers had rejected the manuscript. The American rights were sold only after an editor at Harcourt Brace, working in a Cambridge bookshop to get an idea of the British market, learned of the demand for the sold-out book. It finally appeared in the US in August 1946.

*Animal Farm* is the most familiar allegory of the 20th century, as it represented the 'truth' about historical events. The book has been compared to the satire of Jonathan Swift (1667–1745), author of *Gulliver's Travels* (1726), but unlike Swift's multi-volume, complex allusions, *Animal Farm*'s targets are easily identified by readers with only a passing interest in history or politics.

This was revolution – specifically the Soviet revolution – betrayed. The first stage of the dream of Old Major (Karl Marx) is achieved with the overthrow of the small-time capitalist Mr Jones by the hard-working proletarian animals, but nasty Napoleon (Joseph Stalin) out-manoeuvres Snowball (Leon Trotsky) and takes control, aided by the propaganda of Squealer and the brute force of the dogs. The animals end up labouring for a pig elite: sheep bleat their mindless assent; hens are put on show trial and executed; and the honest, hard-working cart horse, Boxer, is carted off to the glue factory. Not even the anti-capitalist stance remains, as Napoleon and the pigs interact with humans again to the point where it becomes impossible to distinguish pig from human, human from pig. So much for Major's injunction that in the fight against man the animals should never come to resemble him.[257]

The Union of Soviet Socialist Republics (USSR) was formally constituted on 6 July 1923, covering most of the old Russian empire overthrown in the communist revolution of 1917, minus the territories that formed Finland, Poland, the Baltic Republics and East Prussia. With the fall of communism, it collapsed in 1991.

*Animal Farm* is powerful in its simplicity, a power evident in the way it spread as samizdat literature to question Soviet influence in eastern Europe. Yet it remains a simple work. As one shrewd critic noted, *Animal Farm* 'does not begin to cast light on what for any socialist is the real question: what has gone wrong and why?'[258] Orwell would offer the justification, repeated by his followers, that the allegory of 'revolution betrayed' was a vital if painful corrective

The Northern Stage Theatre Company in a scene from *Animal Farm* at the Young Vic, 1997

to a British public opinion besotted with the alleged virtues of its wartime ally. Conveniently, this interpretation establishes Orwell as the virtuous, independent and correct voice challenging the might of establishment opinion.

However, few people in Britain were embracing the Soviet Union as a workers' paradise, especially after the purges of the 1930s, and any image of Moscow as a moral bastion against National Socialism had been shattered by the German–Soviet Non-Aggression Pact of 1939. Rather, as Winston Churchill cogently noted, if Hitler invaded Hell, 'I would make at least a favorable reference to the Devil in the House of Commons.'[259] Heavy-handed maintenance of the wartime alliance did lead to short-sighted – not to mention ethically questionable – actions, such as the government's pressure on Jonathan Cape to reject *Animal Farm*. However, this was far from proof that the communists had not only sabotaged the workers' revolution in the Soviet Union, but could undermine the British state and society.

The reality of communism in Britain was irrelevant, as was any complexity of economic, political or international relations. As early as 1938, Orwell had decided that *the very important question . . .*

is whether a western country can in practice be controlled by Communists acting under Russian orders.[260] The worry that *the English left-wing intelligentsia worship Stalin because they have lost their patriotism and their religious belief without losing the need for a god and a fatherland* would lead Orwell to reiterate in August 1944: *I consider that willingness to criticise Russia and Stalin is the test of intellectual honesty.*[261]

*Animal Farm* carried out this mandate, but, as with his presentation of events in Spain, Orwell's Soviet history is sketchy. The story elides, for example, the Leninist period of 1917–24. Was Lenin simply Stalin before Stalin, betraying the revolution at its inception, or were there several years of hope for the elevation of the proletariat? When Orwell refers to the pigs' dealings with the humans – an allusion culminating in the German–Soviet Pact – is he explicitly condemning Lenin's New Economic Policy of 1921, which allowed some privatisation of property, industry and trade? It is unclear whether Orwell is arguing that any revolution is doomed to betrayal, in which case it can be asserted that the workers should never make the effort in the first place, or whether he is just warning that it is an evil person like Stalin who can take over a good process, in which case communism and some communists might not be so bad after all.

Nor does Orwell offer the possibility of a solution – not even a compromise promising some advance. Witnessing the triumph of Napoleon, should the animals hope for a return to a 'good' capitalist master? Should they seek a new revolution, given the failure of the first one? The suggestion at the end of the novel is that they will helplessly do nothing, accepting their misery in the name of 'progress'.

Writing to the American essayist Dwight Macdonald, Orwell tried to offer a way out: *I meant the moral to be that revolutions only effect a radical improvement when the masses are alert and know how to chuck out their leaders as soon as the latter have done their job . . . What I was* trying to say was, 'You can't have a revolution unless you make it for yourself; there is no such thing as a benevolent dictatorship'.[262] Unfortunately his cherished workers are always helpless. The best animals may be diligent and honest (like Boxer), but they are not smart enough to carry through a successful revolution. When craftier elites like the pigs take over their cause and corrupt it, they can do nothing. Nor was this only a fictional representation: just before *Animal Farm* was published, Orwell wrote of the *semi-anaesthesia in which the British people contrive to live.*[263]

The exalted clarity of Orwell's allegory left it up for grabs. While the first reviewers admired the style of the work, there were numerous alternative interpretations. Some reviewers clashed over whether Orwell's anti-Soviet message was justified, with Kingsley Martin, Orwell's old nemesis at the *New Statesman*, sneering: 'If we read the satire as a jibe at the failings of the USSR and realise that it is historically false and neglectful of the complex truth about Russia, we shall enjoy it and be grateful for our laugh.'[264] Others went further, claiming that Orwell had written a general commentary on the dangers of tyranny and debating his conception of a 'revolution betrayed'. Still others, notably in the US, rejoiced that Orwell was attacking the very concept of socialism.[265]

Had Orwell the socialist meant to condemn socialism? Certainly not, but his basic story had left another opening. It was not clear whether the allegory was only about the specific case of the Soviet Union or a warning that it could happen anywhere. Orwell's concern that the American public would not understand what *Animal Farm* was about was wide of the mark;[266] the issue was whether the book could be appropriated by those, in the US and elsewhere, who wanted to warn people about the 'enemy within'.

In 1945, as in any subsequent year, there was little prospect of a Moscow-led coup in Britain or the US. The Communist Parties in both countries were small and going through internal turmoil.

Those people labelled 'fellow travellers' were usually no more than dissenters questioning aspects of government policy. There were individual spies, on rare occasions in positions of influence, but they hardly constituted a fifth column.

However, with the breakdown of the Grand Alliance of the Second World War and the onset of the Cold War, this did not matter. In a total conflict of communism versus freedom, if the Soviet-fostered threat did not exist, it would have to be created. And, in

The Cold War: the tensions and latent hostilities that characterised the relationship between the Soviet Union and the major western powers, especially the US, following the Second World War. Intensified by the nuclear arms race, the Cold War entered a process of détente in the 1960s with a series of arms reduction and control programmes. The conflict formally ended with the east European revolutions of 1989 and the collapse of the Soviet Union in 1991.

this battle of systems, the threat would have to be created and confronted as much in the cultural arena as in the diplomatic, economic or military spheres. Orwell and *Animal Farm* fitted the bill.

The twist in this tale is that Orwell was far from a fan of the American way of life. In the same 'As I Please' column where he warned *It is difficult to go anywhere in London without having the feeling that Britain is now Occupied Territory*, Orwell satirised the attitudes of the US military in Britain:

[Drunk American] SOLDIER: *Wharrishay is, perfijious Albion. You heard that? Perfijious Albion. Never trust a Britisher. You can't trust the b———s.*

ORWELL: *Can't trust them with what?*

SOLDIER: *Wharrishay is, down with Britain. Down with the British. You wanna do anything 'bout that? Then you can ——— well do it. (Sticks his face out like a tomcat on a garden wall.)* [267]

Orwell's essays – such as his warning in 'Raffles and Miss Blandish' about crude American presentations of crime – went further. As late as November 1946 he was savaging American culture:

*Who, without misgivings, would bring up a child on the coloured 'comics' in which sinister professors manufacture atomic bombs in underground laboratories while Superman whizzes through the clouds, the machine-gun bullets bouncing off his chest like peas, and platinum blondes are raped, or very nearly, by steel robots and 50-foot dinosaurs?* [268]

Orwell had an ill-informed nostalgia for the US of the 19th century. *America before the Civil War may have been a rough place for a man of culture, but it was at any rate a hard country to starve in,* he wrote in one of his first book reviews, and he maintained this position throughout his life. However, just as the 'Golden Country' of England had been spoiled by modern life, so the US had been ruined by *industrialism . . . tightening its grip.* [269]

Orwell might have clarified whether his allegory pointed towards an anti-Soviet alliance with the US – especially after the first reviews indicated he was vanquishing socialism as well as communism – but he was once more enduring tragedy and a forced retreat from public life. While drafting *Animal Farm* he had asked his wife Eileen, for the first time, for her opinion of his work. She never saw the outcome.

In March 1945, while Orwell was in western Germany reporting for the *Observer*, she underwent a hysterectomy, but never emerged from the anaesthetic.

Orwell was now alone with an 11-month-old son, Richard, whom he and Eileen had adopted the previous June. After Eileen's death, he completed his reporting assignment on France, Germany and Austria at the end of the war and returned to Britain to cover the general election, before settling down with Richard. While

Orwell with his son Richard

he still wrote for newspapers, he did not resume his editorship and the 'As I Please' column was suspended until November 1946.

Orwell was unhappy and emotionally unstable. He fell into the habit of proposing marriage to female friends and new acquaintances; he was turned down on at least four occasions. (One of these women was Sonia Brownell, who finally married Orwell just before his death.) The author of *Animal Farm* also had to contend with his deteriorating health. In February 1946 he suffered a haemorrhage in his lungs and was confined to bed for two weeks. He played down the incident, refusing a doctor and continuing some of his weekly writing, but it was an ominous sign of what lay ahead.

Solace for Orwell came in a change of environment. In 1944, he had begun to enquire about renting a farmhouse on Jura, one of the Inner Hebrides off the west coast of Scotland. The arrangements were finally completed in spring 1946 and Orwell arrived at his new home in May.

Orwell's life might be in turmoil, but he had never been more productive. In the year after his wife's death, he wrote more than 130 articles and reviews. Spurred on by the rapidly escalating conflict with the Soviet Union, he was going to stake out his territory in the debate by connecting language, literature and politics.

First, Orwell made his customary division between the 'good' and the 'bad'. In 'Notes on Nationalism' (October 1945) he used 'nationalism' as a catch-all term for those movements he opposed. Hitler's Germany and Stalin's Soviet Union were joined by other less likely candidates such as *Celtic nationalism, neo-Toryism, Zionism, political Catholicism, colour feeling, class feeling* and *pacifism*. Needless to say, Orwell spared his own promotion of England. In his view, nationalism – *the habit of identifying oneself with a single nation or other unit, placing it beyond good and evil and recognising no other duty than that of advancing its interests* – was *not to be confused with patriotism*.[270]

Almost five years after penning *The Lion and the Unicorn*, Orwell was still defining himself *against* things. It is impossible to pin him down on his self-absolution – hadn't he placed England beyond good and evil from 1941? Hadn't he devoted himself to advancing the interests of 'Englishness'? Hadn't he subordinated 'socialism' to that duty? – because he never discussed the 'positive' meaning of patriotism beyond *God Save the King* and the Union Jack.

Orwell was too fixed in his ways to change, but so long as he stayed on the attack, his own position remained beyond examination. He used 'The Prevention of English Literature' (March 1946) to condemn *the poisonous effect of the Russian mythos on English intellectual life,* but a mis-step in this essay exposes Orwell's real position. Having argued that the threat to liberty and writing came not from the right but from the left, he claimed: *The big public do not care about* [liberty] *one way or the other.* Bereft of any positive objective, he could only produce venom for his fellow writers: *The direct, conscious attack on intellectual decency comes from the intellectuals themselves.*[271]

Thus 'Politics and the English Language' (April 1946) moved from the advice that *bad habits* [are] *a necessary step toward political regeneration,* to the castigation of old enemies like the socialist academic Harold Laski (1893–1950), theorists on psychology and communists.[272] An editorial for *Polemic* (May 1946) attacked the scientist J D Bernal (1901–71) – who had accused the journal of 'persistent attempts to confuse moral issues to break down the distinction between right and wrong' – of an assault upon *certain moral and intellectual values whose survival is dangerous from the totalitarian point of view. These are what is loosely called the liberal values – using the word 'liberal' in its old sense of 'liberty-loving'.*[273] 'Politics v. Literature: An Examination of *Gulliver's Travels*' (September–October 1946) balanced the assessment of Jonathan Swift as a *Tory radical* whose *political aims were on the whole reactionary ones* with the reassurance that his *greatest contribution to political thought* [was] *his attack . . . on what would now be called totalitarianism.*[274]

Still Orwell, from belief or from design, avoided being reduced to an anti-communist. Politically, he put some distance between himself and strident American critics of the Soviet Union in his essay 'James Burnham and the Managerial Revolution' (May 1946). Having drawn upon Burnham's model of superstates for his projection of the post-war world, Orwell now salvaged a vestige of hope in a 'third way' by criticising Burnham's *essentially American attitude* and *power worship*, which regarded both a US superpower and a European enemy (be it Germany or the Soviet Union) as inevitable. Both National Socialism and Stalinism, Orwell contended, were doomed to failure through their abolition or democratic transformation.[275]

Even more important was his attempted transcendence of political disputes through the elevation of language and literature. In his broadest autobiographical essay, 'Why I Write' (Summer 1946), Orwell declared his objective: *Every line of serious work that I have written since 1936 has been written, directly or indirectly, against totalitarianism and for democratic socialism*; but he then carried out an aesthetic sleight-of-hand, claiming that what he most wanted to do was *to make political writing into an art*.[276] His argument – combined with essays such as 'Politics and Literature' – is far from subtle. If Orwell's artistry is acknowledged, then his political stance is elevated beyond criticism. Clarity and 'decency' become intertwined, arguably at the expense of a detailed socialism.

Orwell's clarity also obscures other significant features of his political development, the most important of which was his prominent place in an emerging anti-communist network of intellectuals. The supposed foe of 'literary cliques', Orwell actually had influential contacts in the literary world from the 1930s and maintained a range of correspondents from 'working class' writers such as Jack Common (1903–68) to fellow critics of the Spanish Republican government. In London, during the Second World War he was part of a social circle that included writers such as

Anthony Powell (1905–2000), Malcolm Muggeridge (1903–90), and Michael Meyer.

It was in 1943, however, that Orwell began to define a more precise political network among British and European writers. He wrote to Philip Rahv (the editor of the left but anti-communist American journal *Partisan Review*) with a list of possible contributors, from suspect poets such as the Alex Comfort 'crew' to older authors such as E M Forster and writers who were also doing wartime service at the BBC.[277] In 'As I Please', he upheld a school of European political literature which included Italian Ignazio Silone (1900–78), Frenchman André Malraux (1901–76), Austrian Franz Borkenau (1900–57) and Belgian Victor Serge (1890–1947), all of whom wrote against communism, contrasting them with 'poor' English counterparts such as the eternally derided Harold Laski.

Central to this network was the Hungarian emigré Arthur Koestler, who had left eastern Europe and the Communist Party in 1938 and had memorably captured the dilemma of the individual and communism in *Darkness at Noon* (1940). Soon after his

arrival in Britain in 1940, Koestler paid a visit to Orwell, whom he admired as the author of *Homage to Catalonia*. By the end of the war, Koestler was based in north Wales, and Orwell had become a frequent visitor. He would spend Christmas and New Year of 1945–6 with Koestler and his family, including his sister-in-law Celia, who would become an important figure in Orwell's life.

Orwell's supporters have made much of his involvement with

Arthur Koestler

Koestler in the Freedom Defence Committee. It was formed in 1945, with Orwell as vice-chairman, after the prosecution for anti-militarist propaganda of the anarchist newspaper *War Commentary*. Orwell and Koestler also proposed the revival of the League for the Rights of Man for 'psychological disarmament', with free distribution of British newspapers, books and other materials in the Soviet Union.

Orwell's pursuit of freedom in the early months of the Cold War had its merits, but it was only part of the story. It was one matter to defend the rights of an anarchist publication and quite another to support the open promotion of communism, and there was a very thin line between 'psychological disarmament' and 'psychological warfare' against the Soviet Union. Koestler's trajectory is significant: far from maintaining an independent position for freedom, he was soon working with the state, referring anti-communist exiles to US intelligence services.

Wittingly or unwittingly, Orwell was already playing his part in the development of this network. In March 1946, Francis Henson, an American trade unionist, approached Orwell about the work of the International Relief and Rescue Committee (IRRC). Orwell advised Koestler to contact the organisation, and the IRRC was soon asking the emigré to carry out a lecture tour of the US.

From its inception, the IRRC had close links with US officials (later the CIA would provide funding), and the State Department quickly backed Koestler's tour 'as highly desirable in the national interest'. On his three-month journey in spring 1948, Koestler would meet the key members of the anti-communist intelligentsia, including *Partisan Review* editor Philip Rahv, Daniel Bell, Lionel Trilling, Sidney Hook, Mary McCarthy and James Burnham. Through the highly-influential *New Leader*, he met the ex-communist Max Eastman, union leader David Dubinsky, Eugene Lyons and Dwight Macdonald. Many of these acquaintances would join Koestler as founding members of the Congress for Cultural Freedom, developed in 1949 and funded by the CIA as the intellectual vanguard of the 'free world'; Koestler foreshadowed the initiative in a meeting with William Donovan, the wartime director of US intelligence services, where he outlined his ideas for psychological warfare.[278]

Orwell, living in semi-isolation on Jura for much of the year, made fewer high-profile contacts immediately after the war. In some ways, however, his ideas on anti-communism went beyond Koestler's. Contradicting his embrace of quietism in 'Inside the Whale', Orwell criticised Koestler for drawing the conclusion: *This is what revolutions lead to. There is nothing for it except to be a 'short-term pessimist', i.e., to keep out of politics, make a sort of oasis within which you and your friends can remain sane, and hope that somehow things will be better in a hundred years.* He also chided Koestler for his limited castigation of Soviet communism as the corruption of Stalin. In contrast, Orwell believed *all the seeds of evil were there from the start* under Lenin and (interestingly, given Orwell's affiliation with groups such as POUM) Trotsky. He concluded with the pessimistic assessment that there could be no 'pure' revolution, for *in the minds of active revolutionaries, at any rate the ones who 'got there', the longing for a just society has always been fatally mixed up with the intention to secure power for themselves.*[279]

In Orwell's defence, he did make several public stands for a freedom with no strings attached. He was *only very doubtfully pleased* with the wartime suppression of the *Daily Worker* – although he later noted (in a lecture to a working-class audience in favour of the ban): *One is constantly being thrown out in one's judgements because one listens to the articulate minority and forgets the other 99 per cent.*[280] He explained why Indians who broadcast on German radio in the Second World War were not traitors.[281] He defended publication of the poetry of the pacifist Alex Comfort (1920–2000), even though he had vehemently disagreed with the poet in their *Partisan Review* exchange, and he backed the 'Freedom of the Park' after five people were arrested for selling papers in Speakers' Corner in Hyde Park, warning: *The notion that certain opinions cannot safely be allowed a hearing is growing.*[282]

Most prominent in Orwell's campaign for 'freedom' was his reaction to the Duchess of Atholl, who asked him in late 1945 to support the League for European Freedom. In 'As I Please', he had already ridiculed the Duchess as a Tory who backed the communists in 1938 (when they sought a British war against Germany).[283] Now he wrote to her: *I cannot associate myself with an essentially Conservative body which claims to defend democracy in Europe but has nothing to say about British imperialism. It seems to me that one can only denounce the crimes now being committed in Poland, Jugoslavia, etc. if one is equally insistent on ending Britain's unwanted rule in India.*[284]

For all these signs of a general commitment to 'freedom', Orwell was still outlining the limits to be placed on communists in British society. In an essay published in the strident anti-communist pages of *Partisan Review* in summer 1946, Orwell warned that, while the number of open communists and their supporters might be limited, they had assumed importance because of their key positions in society. Trade unions, Parliament and the press were being subverted by the 'Red Menace': *It is a fact that the Communists are at present the main danger to the Government and might become a real political force if some calamity abroad – for example, large-scale fighting in India – made the Government's foreign policy acutely unpopular.* Even when Orwell had calmed his nerves and reassessed the threat, he somehow managed to link communism to the evils not only of the left but of the right: *As open apologists of the Stalin regime, the Communists are now playing on a losing wicket, and yet if they could get inside the Labour Party as an organised body, they might be able to do enormous mischief. Even the worst kind of split could hardly result in a Communist-controlled government, but it might bring back the Conservatives.* [285]

Far from keeping open a broad-church Socialism, Orwell was moving towards an anti-communist 'liberalism', far narrower in its definition of the acceptable. His *Partisan Review* contribution was strikingly similar to essays published at the same time by Arthur Schlesinger Jr, who was defining the 'vital center' in the US between *laissez-faire* capitalism and communism: 'With history breathing down their necks, communists are working overtime to expand party influence, open and covert, in the labor movement, among Negroes, among veterans, among unorganized liberals.'[286] The fight against the supposed menace of subversion rather than the promotion of a new socialist society would take priority.

It was in this context that Orwell was testing the ideas that would fuel his next novel. Compared to his other books, drafting would be slow and measured. By May 1947, he was only a third of the way through a rough draft and was in *most wretched health.*[287] His attention was further distracted by the completion of his bitter essay on his schooldays, 'Such, Such Were the Joys', an appropriate diversion given that Orwell believed *the only English parallel for the nightmare of totalitarianism was the experience of a misfit boy in an English boarding school.*[288]

The completion of *Nineteen Eighty-four* and of Orwell's life were intertwined. Now established in Jura and with fewer distractions from visitors, he made one last effort. He wrote to Fredric Warburg that the manuscript was *a ghastly mess as it stands, but the idea is so good that I could not possibly abandon it.*[289] The rough draft was finished in October 1948, and Orwell collapsed into bed from exhaustion. Weeks later, he entered a hospital near Glasgow, where he remained for seven months.

In hospital Orwell kept a notebook, making notes on alterations for the manuscript. In May, the doctors finally allowed him to resume typing, and in July he returned to Jura. By early November

1948, he had finished the novel and, despite falling ill again, insisted on retyping the final draft. Just before Christmas he admitted to friends *I am really very unwell indeed.*[290] Three weeks later, he was in a sanatorium in Gloucestershire.

*Nineteen Eighty-four* was published by Secker and Warburg on 8 June 1949 in London, and five days later by Harcourt, Brace in New York. Orwell, always downbeat, had written to Warburg: *It isn't a book I would gamble on for a big sale, but I suppose one could be sure of 10,000 anyway.*[291] His publishers were prepared for a major success, however, and within a year

Original jacket of *Nineteen Eighty-four*, published by Secker & Warburg, 1949

almost 50,000 copies had been sold in Britain, 170,000 in the US, and another 190,000 through the Book-of-the-Month Club.

Like *Animal Farm*, the general plot of *Nineteen Eighty-four* is familiar to most people, even those who have not read it. Winston Smith, living in a bleak London of the near-future, is a downtrodden minor bureaucrat in the Ministry of Truth of Oceania, one of three super-states. The population is divided into a majority proletariat, ignorant and trapped in the slums; a smaller section of Outer Party functionaries carrying out the administration of the State (and kept in line by a propaganda that wipes memories and insists on allegiance to Big Brother and by the coercion of the Thought Police); and an Inner Party elite.

When Winston decides to begin a diary, it is a rebellion with a wider significance, for he is trying to recover his memory. This rebel act is intertwined with his evolving relationship with Julia, a young typesetter whose sexual promiscuity is her own rebellion against 'Big Brother', and their introduction to O'Brien, a member

From the 1956 film version of *Nineteen Eighty-four*

of the 'Inner Party'. O'Brien's proposed revolution is a trap leading to the arrest and torture of Winston and Julia. Winston is forced to betray all he holds dear, renouncing his love for Julia and his memory. The novel ends with a mentally broken Winston realising HE LOVED BIG BROTHER.

*Nineteen Eighteen-four* was always going to be a distinctive novel, irrespective of the era in which it appeared. It was a unique vision or, as Orwell put it, *a fantasy . . . in the form of a naturalistic novel.*[292] There were a handful of prominent dystopian novels in the 1920s and 1930s – such as Aldous Huxley's *Brave New World* (1932), H G Wells's *The Shape of Things to Come* (1933) and Evgeny Zamyatin's *We* (1920–1) – but Orwell's world was a future of the here and now. The telescreen was a larger version of the recently invented television; the cinema propaganda was an exaggeration of the newsreels that had been informing audiences for a generation; and substandard items in short supply were all too plausible for a Britain still enduring rationing. Locations such as Trafalgar/Victory Square and institutions like *The Times* were part of everyday British life. Gordon Comstock's modernist London and Winston Smith's 'futurist'

Russian author and playwright Evgeny Zamyatin (1884–1937) is best known for his dystopian novel *We* (*My*), which prophesied Stalinism and the failure of the revolution. It greatly influenced Orwell's *Nineteen Eighty-four*. Zamyatin introduced many western writers to the Soviet Union, but his life was made difficult there after *We* was published abroad. In 1931, he emigrated to Paris.

one were not so very different.

Nineteen Eighty-four was also praised as a significant 'psychological' novel. Beyond its political themes is a depiction, as Orwell wrote in a 1944 essay, of *the cult of power . . . mixed up with a love of cruelty and wickedness for their own sakes.*[294] It was not the first novel to depict mental torture (Zamyatin's *We* covers similar ground), but it is remarkable in that it gives the torturer a human face. The reader is introduced to O'Brien as a possible hero, long before he is revealed as Winston's enemy. Even the division between good and evil is not complete: O'Brien, who succeeds in part because he is admired as well as feared by Winston, breaks down the differences between persecutor and persecuted: *Do you remember writing in your diary that it did not matter whether I was a friend or an enemy, since I was at least a person who understood you and could be talked to? You were right. I enjoy talking to you. Your mind appeals to me. It resembles my own mind except that you happen to be insane.*[295]

*Man only stays human by preserving large patches of simplicity in his life, while the tendency of many modern inventions – in particular, the film, the radio, and the aeroplane – is to weaken his consciousness, dull his curiosity, and, in general, drive him nearer to the animals.*

GEORGE ORWELL, January 1946[293]

This notion of 'power', rather than an application of it to the Cold War, dominated British reviews of the book. Veronica Wedgwood in *Time and Tide* explained: 'It is no doubt with the intention of preventing his prediction from coming true that Mr Orwell has set it down in the most valuable, the most absorbing, the most powerful book he has yet written.'[296] V S Pritchett in the *New Statesman* compared the work to the best of Swift as a pointed depiction of the 'moral corruption of absolute power', and Julian Symons in the *Times Literary Supplement* offered 'thanks for a writer . . . who is able to speak seriously and with originality of the nature of reality and the terrors of power'.[297] A slight discordant note came from the American critic Diana Trilling: while she thought the portrayal 'brilliant and fascinating', 'the nature of its fantasy [was] so absolutely final and relentless' that she could 'recommend it only with a certain reservation'.[298]

This battle for control of the mind is part of Orwell's broader concern with language, embodied in the comment of Winston's eager co-worker: *It's a beautiful thing, the destruction of words.*[299] The desecration of language in turn is part of the destruction of memory and 'history', represented by the antique coral hemisphere that Winston purchases in the 'junk' shop in the prole sector. Orwell had considered this in other novels, crudely in *A Clergyman's Daughter*, much more richly and thoughtfully in *Coming Up for Air*, but never in the context of the system's attempt to control, manufacture and even obliterate memory. Pre-war conceptions of the 'Golden Country' and terrors of betrayal and loss interact with a sketch of propaganda to offer the full portrayal of Winston Smith's struggle. As he concludes: *If the Party could thrust its hand into the past and say of this or that event, it never happened – that, surely, was more terrifying than mere torture and death?*[300]

There are other, less attractive aspects of *Nineteen Eighty-four* that can be seen as the culmination of Orwell's sharpening vision. Foremost among these is misogyny. Katherine, Winston's wife, is reduced to a frigid slave of 'Party' doctrine. Julia, Katherine's opposite, is amoral and wilfully ignorant, a woman for whom *everything came back to her sexuality.*[301] Winston's first thoughts of Julia are of rape and conquest: *He would flog her to death with a rubber truncheon. He would tie her naked to a stake and shoot her full of arrows like Saint Sebastian. He would ravish her and cut her throat at the moment of climax.*[302] Even when Julia's one positive quality of 'love' for Winston is established, it is undercut by the depiction of her as *a rebel from the waist down*. The caricature is so stark that, when Winston betrays Julia by urging O'Brien to turn the rats on her, it is a betrayal not of her but of Winston's benevolence towards a flawed companion.

Julia is balanced – as in an angel–whore complex[303] – by

Winston's sainted mother. She is the archetype of sacrifice, giving herself up for Winston even though, with the stealing of the chocolate from his sister, he is revealed to be unworthy. Slain by both the repression of the 'State' and the greed of her son, her essential goodness is expressed not through intellectual depth but through the simple picture of maternal care for her children. (In contrast, Julia with the *shapeliness of her hips, supple waist,* and *body gleam*[ing] *white in the sun* is removed from the maternal by Winston's conclusion that *out of their bodies no child would ever come*.)[304]

Between these two images of Winston's mother and his lover is the 'prole' washerwoman. Initially, she is described as *a monstrous woman*,[305] but Orwell eventually presents her as *beautiful*, with the maternal image of *strong arms, a warm heart, and a fertile belly*.[306] Of course, Orwell, through Winston, has not actually seen the light about his women; the portrayals at each extreme are patronising caricatures.

Yet, rightly or wrongly, all these dimensions of *Nineteen Eighty-four* are secondary to its place in the escalating contest with the Soviet Union. This significance was enhanced by the unusually long time it took to write. When Orwell began the novel, conflict with Moscow was still on a case-by-case basis over issues like the future of Germany. By the time the first draft was completed, the show-down had gone global with the challenge of the Truman Doctrine that 'nearly every nation must choose between alternative ways of life'.[307] And before the submission of the final manuscript, the situation would become critical with the communist-led coup in Czechoslovakia, tension over France and Italy and their role in the Marshall Plan, and the start of the Berlin Blockade.

Ironically, when *Nineteen Eighty-four* finally appeared in June 1949, the worst of the crisis in Europe had passed. The Berlin Blockade finally ended in May, and an eyeball-to-eyeball stability was in place. The struggle was moving to other areas, however. The communists of Mao Zedong (1893–1976) were about to take control of China, and the image of American military superiority would be shattered in September by confirmation that the Soviet Union had exploded an atomic bomb.

Most importantly, the crusade against communism was being waged at home. Long before Senator Joseph McCarthy (1908–57) waved his piece of paper and claimed that dozens, if not hundreds, of 'Reds' had infiltrated the US government, the search for subversives and 'fellow travellers' had begun. Partly from fear, partly from the quest for global advantage, and partly to assure electoral victory in 1948, President Truman's staff had advised: 'Every effort must be made now to jointly and at one and the same time – although, of course, by different groups, to dissuade [Henry Wallace, the presidential candidate of the Progressive Party] and also identify him and isolate him in the public mind with the communists.'[308] Every sector of American society would be affected by the purge of suspect left-wingers: trade unions, professional bodies, academic staff, youth and women's groups, African-American organisations, journalists, and film and television companies would all be 'cleansed'.

Britain had its own less virulent variety of McCarthyism. Despite the prophecies of the most strident American Cold Warriors, there was never any prospect that British socialism would lead to communism – key figures in the Labour government such as Ernest Bevin (1881–1951) had fought running battles with communists in trade unions since the 1920s – but the Attlee government was going to pursue a subtler campaign than that of its American counterpart against the threat.

In January 1948, the British cabinet, in a comprehensive review of policy and operations at the outset of the Cold War, established a specialist unit called the Information Research Department (IRD). The IRD was never officially recognised; instead it worked in a 'grey' area between British intelligence services, the Foreign Office and private allies. It would disseminate anti-communist material through all possible media. From IRD-supplied material, journalists would publish articles, trade unions would produce newsletters, authors would write books, the BBC would develop radio scripts. The only condition for use was that the source of the material never be identified.[309]

*Nineteen Eighty-four*'s special contribution to this cultural crusade was its presentation, in Orwell's words, of *totalitarian ideas* [that] *have taken root in the minds of intellectuals everywhere . . . to draw these ideas out to their logical consequences.*[310] 'Totalitarianism', at the time of the novel, was only beginning to be analysed by specialists inside and outside government, and the first book-length examination arrived only in 1951 with Hannah Arendt's *The Origins of Totalitarianism*.

Culturally, however, the term was already widespread. Applied retrospectively to the National Socialist regime in Germany, its political force came through the labelling of the contemporary Soviet Union. President Truman declared in May 1947: 'There isn't any difference in totalitarian states. I don't care what you call them, Nazi, Communist or Fascist.'[311] The notion of 'Red Fascism' had become a powerful justification for a US foreign policy of confrontation with Moscow.

Unlike *Animal Farm*, *Nineteen Eighty-four* was not written as an allegory of the Soviet system or even a communist one. There were considerable problems with such an interpretation. Not only was the story set in London, but Oceania was clearly modelled on an American superstate. Orwell's naming of Britain as 'Airstrip One' would be adopted later by those criticising subservience to the US.

Nor had Orwell attributed the rise of totalitarianism to the success of a communist 'enemy within'. Instead *Nineteen Eighty-four* seemed to indicate that, given the nature of power and its use of technology, communism was not the issue; any society was inherently vulnerable to the centralised exertion of authority by the few over the many. Such an interpretation was not only a precursor of Arendt's work, it was remarkably similar to the Frankfurt School, whose concern was with the tensions and contradictions within capitalist 'democracy'.[312]

Orwell (unlike Arendt and the Frankfurt School) had at times drifted into a general explanation of power as *largely non-rational*.[313] He returned, however, to the rational use of technology by the 'super-states', not to destroy each other but to repress their own populations. In 'You and the Atom Bomb' (printed less than three months after the strikes on Hiroshima and Nagasaki), Orwell envisaged a world ruled by *three great empires, each self-contained and cut off from contact with the outer world* [in] *an epoch as horribly stable as the slave empires of antiquity*.[314] To this extent, there was no inherent moral superiority of the west over the Soviet Union.

Those fighting the Cold War were not bothered by such nuances; as Orwell's publisher Fredric Warburg had privately commented: 'Here is the Soviet Union to the *n*th degree, a Stalin who never dies, a secret police with every device of modern technology.'[315] In the promotion of *Nineteen Eighteen-four* by the Cold Warriors, the 'Party' of Oceania was the Communist Party of 1948, and that was that. As a newspaper vendor told the author Isaac Deutscher: 'You must read this book, sir. Then you will know why we must drop the atomic bomb on the Bolshies.'[316] Harcourt Brace, the American publishers of *Nineteen Eighty-four*, did nothing to correct such assumptions; rather, it used them to market the book. In April 1949 they approached J Edgar Hoover, the head of the Federal Bureau of Investigation (FBI), for an endorsement: 'We hope you might be interested in helping to call this book to the attention of the American public – and thus, perhaps, helping to halt totalitarianism.'[317]

The reviewer for the *New York Times* proclaimed the book 'a great work of kinetic art', for 'no other work of this generation has made us desire freedom more earnestly or loathe tyranny with such fulness'.[318] Philip Rahv of *Partisan Review* announced: 'This novel is the best antidote to the totalitarian disease that any writer has so far produced ... I recommend it particularly to those liberals who still cannot get over the political superstition that while absolute power is bad when exercised by the right, it is in its very nature good and a boon to humanity once the left, that is to say "our own people", takes hold of it.'[319]

When interpretations in *Time* and *Life* magazines extended to 'threats' such as the Labour Party, Orwell was forced to respond: *My recent novel is NOT intended as an attack on Socialism or on the British Labour Party (of which I am a supporter) but as a show-up of the perversions to which a centralised economy is liable and which have already been partly realised in Communism and Fascism. I do not believe that the kind of society I describe necessarily will arrive, but I believe . . . that something resembling it could arrive.*[320]

Unfortunately, Orwell had already undermined his position. His choice of 'Ingsoc' (English Socialism) to describe the political philosophy of Oceania's 'Party' was read not as an example of the corruption of socialist ideals, but as a warning of the ultimate goal of socialism. Warburg had commented when he first read the manuscript: 'This I take to be a deliberate and sadistic attack on socialism and socialist parties generally . . . It seems to indicate a final breach between Orwell and socialism, not the socialism of equality and human brotherhood which clearly Orwell no longer expects from socialist parties, but the socialism of Marxism and the managerial revolution.'[321]

The 'negative' attacks on the left and socialism could not be countered by a 'positive' alternative, for Orwell once more had written a book that 'offered no way out of our century's ordeals'.[322]

John Hurt as Winston Smith in the 1984 film version of *Nineteen Eighty-four*

*Nineteen Eighty-four* does not need a happy ending (as in the US film version which ends with Winston and Julia overcoming their conditioning and defying the 'State/Party' as they are gunned down); the power of the novel comes from its depiction of the individual being crushed by the system. Rather, the issue was: for whom is the revolution being fought? The 'common man' of *The Lion and The Unicorn* is a travesty in *Nineteen Eighty-four*, making a mockery of Winston's declaration: *If there is hope, it lies in the proles.*[323]

Winston sets out the task ahead for the proles: *Until they become conscious they will never rebel, and until after they have rebelled they cannot become conscious*; but the book frequently offers the mantra *It makes no difference.*[324] The working class, far from being empowered or even ennobled in *Nineteen Eighty-four*, are either good-hearted but passive, or threatening and irrational, such as the old prole in the pub who can offer *nothing but a rubbish-heap of details* to Winston.[325] Not one person shows intelligence or considered thought. Richard

Rees, Orwell's long-time benefactor and admirer, confessed: 'What is pathetic . . . in both *Animal Farm* and *Nineteen Eighty-four* is the helpless, inert, and almost imbecile role which [Orwell] attributes to the common man.'[326] The reader is left with the consolation of the poor but happy washerwoman, but as Beatrix Campbell notes, Orwell 'excludes the working class from history and fails to give them any place in the revolutionary cast, other than the supporting role, the proverbial extras.'[327]

In the end we are left with two options regarding Orwell's almost 20 years of 'documenting' the working class. Either he admits that it has all been a cruel joke, for there is no way of elevating the proles, or he has given the reader an idealised caricature, pure in heart and hard in labour, which somehow compensates for the degraded reality in the pub and the street. It is like waiting for Dick Van Dyke's chirpy cockney in *Mary Poppins* to start a revolution.

Some of Orwell's defenders have fallen back on the position that the principle of the individual rebelling against an unjust system is sufficient, even if that rebellion ends in failure. Others have evaded the question of failure by contending that the novel is simply a warning of what might happen if each of us does not remain vigilant. In short, the lesson of *Nineteen Eighty-four* is a 'freedom' untainted by any broader political philosophy.

It's a nice touch, as it gets around those questions of equality, fairness and opportunity that might distract a socialist. *Nineteen Eighty-four* can now be presented as a Cold War tract, since the issue is that 'we' have freedom and 'they' haven't. Just after he had finished this book-length warning about serving 'Big Brother', Orwell was doing exactly that, co-operating with the secret services of the British state.

In the Second World War, Orwell began keeping a list of people he suspected of being Nazi sympathisers. The list, kept in a pale blue notebook, soon evolved into a catalogue of those who might be too close to the Soviet Union or communism. Arthur Koestler encouraged the project and may have annotated the list.

Lying in a Gloucestershire sanitorium in March 1949, Orwell mentioned his list to a special visitor, Koestler's sister-in-law Celia Paget, now Celia Kirwan, who had been the target of his affections a few years earlier. Soon after they had met at Koestler's home in Christmas 1945, Orwell had proposed to her. Kirwan 'gently refused him', but they remained close friends.[328] Now she had a professional as well as a personal interest in seeing Orwell, for she was working for the top-secret Information Research Department, created in 1948 to disseminate anti-communist propaganda throughout Britain and overseas.[329]

While visiting Orwell, Kirwan just happened to mention her work with the IRD. 'He was delighted to learn of them,' she reported back, 'and expressed his wholehearted and enthusiastic approval of our aims.' Orwell's failing health prevented him from writing for the IRD, but he did suggest names of others who might be of use. Kirwan 'left some material with [Orwell]', with a view to sending 'photostats of some of his articles on the theme of Soviet repression of the arts, in the hope that he may become inspired when he is better to take them up again'.[330]

A week later, Orwell asked Richard Rees to retrieve a notebook from his bedroom at his London flat. He considered the list throughout April, writing Rees on 2 May about some of the names: 'The whole difficulty is to decide where each person stands, & one has to treat each case individually.' He had already decided, however, and on the same day he sent Kirwan a list of 36 names.[331]

Orwell's original list had 105 names. The British government still refuses to release the names of the chosen 36, and Orwell's notebook is withheld from public view.[332] The 'known' suspects include Labour MPs; the future Poet Laureate, Cecil Day-Lewis; actor Michael Redgrave; actor and director Orson Welles; actor and singer Paul Robeson; and the historians Isaac Deutscher and A J P Taylor. American novelist John Steinbeck made Orwell's list as a *Spurious Writer*.

Although many of those named were known to Orwell only by their alleged reputations, he included some figures from his past. He might have warmed to Stephen Spender after meeting him, but Spender was still noted as a *Sentimental sympathiser, & very unreliable. Easily influenced. Tendency towards homosexuality.* Charlie Chaplin had been admired by Orwell in 1941 for *his power to stand for a sort of concentrated essence of the common man, for the ineradicable belief in decency that exists in the hearts of ordinary people*; but now he put two question marks by his name.[333] In one of his earliest book reviews, Orwell had praised J B Priestley for his *frank optimism*.[334] Now he was not only a *Strong sympathiser* with *possibly . . . some kind of*

Clockwise from top left: Michael Redgrave, John Steinbeck, J B Priestley, Richard Crossman and Paul Robeson, among Orwell's 105 names

ORWELL'S LIST

*organisational tie-up* and *Very anti-USA*, but he had made *huge sums of money in* [the] *USSR*.

Richard Crossman, the Labour MP and psychological warfare veteran of the Second World War, was noted in Orwell's list as a *Political climber. Zionist (appears sincere about this.) Too dishonest to be outright F.T.* (i.e., fellow traveller). In a wonderful irony, however, Crossman would soon be commissioned to write suitable material for the IRD. Similarly Harold Laski, Orwell's long-time nemesis, received a special pencilled entry: *LASKI!*, even though Laski had been approvingly quoted by Cold Warriors such as Arthur Schlesinger, Jr for his comment that 'the Communist Parties outside Russia act without moral scruples, intrigue without any sense of shame, are utterly careless of truth, sacrifice, without any hesitation, the means they use to the ends they serve. The result is a corruption, both of the mind and of the heart, which is alike contemptuous of reason and careless of truth.'[335] The IRD overlooked Orwell's warning and employed Laski to write a piece comparing British trade unionism favourably with its Soviet counterpart.[336]

There is another wonderfully curious twist in the Orwell-Kirwan exchange. Victor Gollancz may or may not have been on Orwell's list, but Orwell rehabilitated the publisher, with all his supposed communist tendencies, in conversation. According to Kirwan's report to the IRD: 'Mr Orwell said that undoubtedly Gollancz would be the man to publish such a series of books as we had in mind. He would have been very willing to act as a go-between if he had been well enough; as it was, he would try to think of someone else who would do so . . . He said that Gollancz books always sell well, and that they are well displayed and given the widest publicity.'[337]

The annotations to the list indicate that it was not a simple catalogue of denunciation. Some figures are confirmed as *Sympathiser Only* and *Appeaser Only*. Day-Lewis was evaluated as *Previously C.P.*

[Communist Party] *Probably not now completely reliable,* and Deutscher *Could change??*

Orwell's comments make clear that this was far more than a 'party game', as Richard Rees later claimed. It was a considered attempt by Orwell – and whoever annotated the list – to establish those who were clearly beyond Cold War acceptability and those who were merely *stupid, naive, insincere,* or *dishonest.* As Orwell wrote to Kirwan, enclosing the 36 names: *It isn't a bad idea to have the people who are probably unreliable listed.*[338]

Orwell's list and his relationship with the IRD should also be considered in a wider, more 'positive' light. In addition to Gollancz, Orwell offered the names of other writers and journalists who might be of assistance. These included Gleb Struve and Franz Borkenau, whose anti-communist work had been favourably reviewed by Orwell since the experience of Spain. Orwell also recommended *hordes of Americans, whose names can be found in the* New Leader, *the Jewish monthly paper* Commentary, *& the* Partisan Review.[339] In effect, he was assisting the British state in the development of a network to fight the Cold War for 'hearts and minds'. He had good company: the same process of defining 'good' and 'bad' writers, artists, politicians and others was being undertaken in the US – less dramatically, but well in advance of Senator Joseph McCarthy's allegations against 'Red infiltration' – by intellectuals and activists such as Arthur Schlesinger, Jr, Sidney Hook, James Burnham and Eleanor Roosevelt, as well as President Truman and his advisors.

As long as both the British government and the Orwell Archive withhold the 36 names, the full significance of Orwell's action cannot be evaluated. Nevertheless, after the revelation in the press of the Orwell-Kirwan meeting in 1996, the author's defenders queued up to offer a variety of explanations: Orwell was ill and/or he was in love with Celia Kirwan; the list was just a bit of fun;

the list was a serious compilation of naive/devious/treacherous individuals; the list was intended to help the British government find out who was unreliable if approached for assistance; the IRD was not part of the British intelligence services; Orwell was right to draw up the list because the Soviets were a serious threat in 1949 and, even if they were not a threat, they could have been, and even if they were not a threat and could not have been, people thought they were.[340]

Such explanations are inadequate, if not misleading, because they are tied to Orwell's personal and political circumstances in 1949. Far from being a one-off indiscretion, Orwell's list is the culmination of his response to the left from the 1930s onwards. Not only could he not co-operate with many fellow writers and activists, not only did he denigrate them publicly and privately, but he maintained a watch on them as possible subversives.

Even while he kept his list, Orwell supported the cases of those threatened by suppression or prosecution. A few weeks before Kirwan's visit, he wrote to Richard Rees: *I always disagree when people end by saying that we can only combat Communism, Fascism, or what not if we develop an equal fanaticism. It appears to me that one defeats the fanatic precisely by not being a fanatic oneself, but on the contrary by using one's intellect.*[341] He agreed, with some misgivings, to sign a petition protesting the conviction of the scientist Alan Nunn May, accused of espionage for the Soviet Union, because the sentence of ten years was too harsh and *the less spy-hunting is indulged in, the better.*[342] On more than one occasion he opposed a ban on the Communist Party.[343]

However, Orwell's dispute was not with the aims of anti-communists but with their methods. He objected that, while *there are times when it is justifiable to suppress a political party*, outlawing communist political activity would give comfort to those right-wingers *who would approve.*[94] He was uncomfortable with the open display of state power, as *the way in which the Government seems to be going to work is vaguely disquieting, and the whole phenomenon seems to me part of the general breakdown of the democratic outlook.*[345]

Orwell seems to have had no problem with more subtle monitoring of those with dubious beliefs and the passing of information between concerned citizens and their government. He was ever vigilant against threats such as Harold Laski: when a Ukrainian refugee asked for some of Laski's publications, Orwell warned, *Have nothing to do with Laski and by no means let a person of that type know that illicit printing in Soviet languages is going on in the allied zones.*[346] When Dwight Macdonald sent him a book on Henry Wallace, Orwell responded: *Very good, and I am urging Gollancz to publish it over here. I am afraid Wallace may well cause 'our' man* [Truman] *to lose the election, and then Lord knows what may happen.*[347]

In a letter to George Woodcock, Orwell tried to establish a guideline for anti-communist activity: *It is a matter of distinguishing between a real and merely theoretical threat to democracy, and no one should be persecuted for expressing his opinions, however antisocial, and no political organisation suppressed, unless it can be shown that there is a substantial threat to the stability of the state.*[348] This goal, however, fell away before his passionate hatred of foes on the left. In January 1947, Konni Zilliacus, a Labour MP who advocated co-operation with the Soviet Union, tested Orwell by demanding to know if he was calling him a clandestine member of the Communist Party. Orwell offered no evidence that Zilliacus was a *crypto-Communist*, but merely noted: *If what I have suggested is obviously untrue, why does he get so hot and bothered about it?* The legal and political defence of freedom had given way to guilt by association: *What I believe, and will go on believing until I see evidence to the contrary, is that* [Zilliacus] *and others like him are pursuing a policy barely distinguished from that of the CP* [Communist Party], *and that they are in effect the publicity agents of the USSR in this country . . . I could not prove that in a court of law any more than I could have proved before the war that the Catholic Church was sympathetic to Fascism.*[349]

The plausible explanation for Orwell's sustained assault on those he deemed 'unreliable' is that he had no alternative. He could not or would not reclaim a positive conception of socialism. Instead, he complained that *political behaviour is largely non-rational,* and that *the world is suffering from some kind of mental disease which must be diagnosed before it can be cured.* He hoped his adopted son would become a farmer so that he could escape the threat of the atomic bomb, which Orwell expected would be dropped on cities.[350]

In place of a socialist vision, Orwell offered a notion of liberalism removed from any specific economic or political objectives. In 'Writers and Leviathan' (1948) he wrote: *What kind of State rules over us must depend partly on the prevailing intellectual atmosphere: meaning, in this context, partly on the attitude of writers and artists themselves, and on their willingness or otherwise to keep the spirit of liberalism alive.* He ruled out socialism by reducing left-wing thought to a *perfectionist ideology* (with *a whole series of unadmitted contradictions*), embodied in the problems of the Russian revolution and the dependence of any British version upon the exploitation of its colonies. Indeed, any political movement was now unacceptable to Orwell, since *acceptance of any political discipline seems to be incompatible with literary integrity.* He could only make a general call for the freedom of the author *as an individual, an outsider, at the most an unwelcome guerrilla on the flank of a regular army.*[351]

Still, there was a moment when Orwell might have offered his readers an 'Ingsoc' that went beyond the derided and decayed variety in *Nineteen Eighty-four.* In 'Toward European Unity' (1947) he had announced that *democratic Socialism must be made to work throughout some large area.* More importantly, Orwell provided, for the first and only time, his vision of a 'Third Force'. With North America caught up in capitalism and the Soviet Union in the grip of the Communist Party, this socialism must come from a *federation of the western European states*, without their colonial dependencies.[352]

Significantly Orwell's article, for once, was in accord with the thoughts of the Attlee government. Britain might have been allied with the US in the defence of western Europe against the perceived threat of Soviet expansion, but the government did not see the alliance as an unbreakable shackle to American capitalism. In January 1948, the cabinet agreed 'to develop our power and influence to equal that of the United States of America and the USSR . . . We should be able to carry out our task in such a way which will show clearly that we are not subservient to the United States or to the Soviet Union.' Prime Minister Clement Attlee told the nation in a radio broadcast: 'Our task is to work out a system of a new and challenging kind, which combines individual freedom with a planned economy, democracy with social justice.'[353]

This window of opportunity would be open only briefly, however. Beset by continued economic problems, Britain would be tied into the American-led system underwritten by the Marshall Plan and culminating in the formation of the North Atlantic Treaty Organisation (Nato). The devaluation of the pound by 33 per cent against the dollar in 1949 ended any dream of a 'Third Force'.

And Orwell's own idea was set aside as well. In May 1948, again writing for an American journal, he offered a synopsis of Britain's 'Struggle for Survival'. The article has been upheld by some critics as the best approximation of 'a full-blooded endorsement of British Labourism and its reformist politics',[354] but it is better read as a return to Orwellian pessimism. He expressed disappointment that the Attlee government had not brought fundamental changes in British society – although he refrained from saying what those fundamental changes should be – and resigned himself to the notion that any socialist principles would give way to the fight for

Sonia Brownell,
Orwell's second wife

economic survival. Significantly, he closed with the charge that he had levelled against socialism in the 1930s: there was a fundamental contradiction between a high standard of living and the exalted principle of decolonisation.[355]

In April 1949, Orwell underwent another course of treatment to check the tuberculosis. The experimental drug streptomycin had worked the previous year, but this time the results were *ghastly*.[356] He was moved from the Gloucestershire sanatorium to University College Hospital, London, his last hope being complete rest.

Orwell fulfilled one wish in October when he and Sonia Brownell were married in a special ceremony in University College Hospital. His health improved temporarily after the wedding, but gradually Sonia took over his correspondence. Plans were made for a stay in a Swiss sanatorium, but on 21 January 1950, just before the scheduled departure, he died suddenly of a lung haemorrhage. He was 46 years old.

In the end, Orwell's crusade, like Winston Smith's, had been that of a lone liberal. In the end, it was doomed to failure. He wrote to T R Fyvel: *This stupid war is coming off in abt 10–20 years, & this country will be blown off the map whatever happens. The only hope is to have a home with a few animals in some place not worth a bomb.*[357] A review of Oscar Wilde's *The Soul of Man under Socialism* (1891) became a platform for Orwell's benediction: *Socialism, in the sense of economic collectivism, is conquering the earth at a speed that would hardly have seemed possible 60 years ago, and yet Utopia, at any rate Wilde's Utopia, is no nearer . . . The trouble with the transitional periods is that the harsh outlook which they generate tends to become permanent.*[358]

Yet Orwell the man – as opposed to Orwell the socialist – would succeed. He had become part of a far different network, one whose primary aim, rather than being *for* anything, was standing against not only communism but any other left-wing movement. As T R Fyvel enshrined his friend for the cause: 'The word "saintly" was used by one of his friends and critics after his death, and – well – perhaps he had a touch of this quality.'[359]

The American and British governments worked with this network to ensure the 'right' Orwell was constructed for the Cold War. In 1947, *Animal Farm* was published in a special edition for displaced Ukrainians, most of whom were anti-Soviet and some of whom would join the US-led effort to destabilise the communist bloc. The IRD developed an *Animal Farm* comic strip, which was distributed by British embassies and published in countries such as India, Burma, Eritrea, Thailand, Mexico, Venezuela and Brazil. When *Animal Farm* was reissued in an illustrated edition in 1954, Christopher Woodhouse helpfully reviewed it for the *Times Literary Supplement*: 'There is a long way to go yet; but there is a long time

**DŽ. ORVELS**

# DZĪVNIEKU FARMA

A Latvian translation of
*Animal Farm*, 1954

ahead too. *Animal Farm* will not, like *Uncle Tom's Cabin*, contribute to changing history within a decade or so, but it probably has as good a chance as any contemporary work of winning its author a place – unacknowledged, of course – among Shelley's legislators of the world . . . If the worst comes to the worst and [Orwell] fails as a legislator, he is then virtually certain of immortality as a prophet.'[360] The *Times Literary Supplement* did not mention that Woodhouse was an officer in MI6, the British overseas intelligence service.[361]

Indeed, US intelligence officers would reward Orwell's offer of co-operation in 1949 by putting his work on the cinema screen. Soon after his death, the CIA obtained the film rights to *Animal Farm* from Orwell's widow, Sonia, who met them on the condition that she be introduced to the actor Clark Gable.[362] The American Committee for Cultural Freedom (a 'private' group secretly funded by the CIA) provided advice on the screenplay for *Nineteen Eighty-four*. In 1954, *Animal Farm* was released as an animated feature (the FBI declared that it 'hit the jackpot');[363] the film *1984* appeared two years later.[364]

Eric Blair was dead, but 'George Orwell' was very much alive.

# 'Orwell'

It is, after all, no small thing to have the greatest political writer of this age on one's side; it gives confidence, authority, and weight to one's own political views.

NORMAN PODHORETZ[365]

Since his death in 1950, George Orwell has received more academic and popular attention than any other British writer of the 20th century. His work is regarded as a standard source for authoritative comment about politics and ideology, but also 'culture'. As Alan Brown has noted: 'It is characteristic of the "Orwell" persona that it conveys a neutral, received wisdom of "objective" and "human" truths.'[366] This use of Orwell, however, is not due to any desire to commemorate the author as a literary figure. Instead, it is prompted by Orwell's central position in the political and cultural context of the Cold War and by the promotion of him as an archetypal representative of 'Englishness'.

This process began with the immediate reaction to Orwell's death less than a year after the publication of *Nineteen Eighty-four*. Orwell's literary talents were sidelined in order to celebrate his transcendent morality. Stephen Spender (either forgiving of or oblivious to Orwell's protracted assault on his reputation) lauded him as 'an Innocent, a kind of English Candide of the 20th century. The Innocent is ordinary because he accepts the value of ordinary human decency; he is not a mystic, or a poet.'[367] Tom Hopkinson's clever tribute – 'I know only two present-day works of fiction before which the critic abdicates; one is Arthur Koestler's *Darkness at Noon*, the other Orwell's *Animal Farm*'[368] – cast Orwell's legacy in the terms of the Cold War. Other eulogists did the same, but less subtly. Julian Symons tried to stretch Orwell across classes and time periods, citing his faith in 'the revolutionary power of the proletariat' while calling him 'an Edwardian, even a Victorian' figure 'whose unorthodoxy was valuable in an age of power worship'.[369] Arthur Koestler lauded his friend and political ally as 'the only writer of genius among the *littérateurs* of social revolt between the two wars', but V S Pritchett (who had criticised Orwell in 1938) came up with the image that would place the author as first among socialist equals: 'George Orwell was the wintry conscience of a generation which in the thirties had heard the call to the rasher assumptions of political faith.'[370]

In the US, Orwell's death was opportune for those who were constructing the 'vital center' against perceived enemies at home and abroad. He was most effectively claimed by the essayist and critic Lionel Trilling, who wrote the introduction to an American edition of *Homage to Catalonia* (which finally appeared in 1951). Trilling had established himself as the spokesman for the moral middle way, and he represented Orwell as a fellow resident of this hallowed ground. Orwell told the truth 'in an exemplary way, quietly, simply, with due warning to the reader that it was only one man's truth'. It was here that 'St George' was canonised: 'It is hard to find personalities in the contemporary world who are analogous to Orwell. We have to look for men who have considerable intellectual power but who are not happy in the institutionalized life of intellectuality; who have a feeling for an older and simpler time, and a guiding awareness of the ordinary life of the people, yet without any touch of the sentimental malice of populism; and a strong feeling for the commonplace; and a direct, unabashed sense of the nation, even a conscious love of it.'[371]

Amid the eulogies to this moral icon there were a few dissonant voices. Curiously, one of them was another bastion of Englishness, *The Times*, which printed an obituary implying that Orwell had sacrificed his literary ambitions for the mantle of political conscience: 'Though he made his widest appeal in the form of fiction, Orwell had a critical rather than imaginative endowment of mind and he has left a large number of finely executed essays. In a less troubled, less revolutionary period of history he might perhaps have discovered within himself a richer and more creative power of imagination, a deeper philosophy of acceptance. As it was, he was essentially the analyst, by turns indignant, satirical and prophetic, of an order to life and society in rapid dissolution.'[372]

Orwell's admirers had no need to worry, however. The moral perspective continued to dominate from book-length exaltations to radio tributes. John Atkins opened his 1954 study with the words 'The common element in all George Orwell's writing was a sense of decency', and went on to explain that 'the special connotation of this English word is a complex of English living and English attitudes'. He even took up Orwell's battles with other socialists: 'The intellectuals would not revert to [this] sense of decency.'[373] George Woodcock could not bring himself to embrace Orwell as a fellow socialist, but he could praise him as 'a survivor of the free-fighting liberals of the 19th century, a partisan of the values which men like Emerson, Thoreau and Dickens strove to maintain'. For the BBC's appreciation in 1955, Richard Peters (Orwell's student in 1930) observed: 'Was not this the core of George Orwell – a lonely, courageous figure passing with detached honesty and without rancour across the mudbanks of corruption?'[374] Orwell even made an impression behind the Iron Curtain. In *The Captive Mind* (1953), Czeslaw Milosz wrote that *Ninety Eighty-four* was known to certain members of the ruling Communist Party in Poland, for 'Orwell fascinates them through his insight'.[375]

Amid all this praise, any criticism of Orwell's politics could be dismissed as the rambling of Marxist cranks, such as the gripe by British historian A L Morton that 'Nineteen Eighty-four is, for this country at least, the last word to date in counter-revolutionary apologetics'.[376] More thoughtful commentaries were also set aside, including the measured reception in the US of Homage to Catalonia by critics such as the New Republic's George Mayberry ('Orwell's enthusiastic vision of an egalitarian socialism might have been paired with a recognition of the fact that the "road to socialism is paved with bedbugs"') and the Nation's Herbert Matthews ('the danger in this case is that Orwell was writing in a white heat about a confused, unimportant and obscure incident in the Spanish Civil War').[377]

A greater challenge emerged as critics turned their attention to Orwell's fiction. Having praised Orwell's politics, Irving Howe had to admit that Nineteen Eighty-four 'is not, I suppose, really a novel, or at least it does not satisfy those expectations we have come to have with regard to the novel'.[378] John Wain was crisper in his criticism: 'Orwell's essays are obviously much better than his novels.'[379]

Even devoted admirers of Orwell preferred not to highlight his skills as a novelist. Stephen Spender sought comfort in the observation that 'he had a kind of quality about him that reminded one of plain living, bread and cheese, English beer, and so on', while Anthony Powell focused on Orwell's courage and friendship 'for whom you felt a curiously protective affection'.[380] In 1956, when Christopher Hollis attempted to treat Orwell not as a biographical subject but as a writer worthy of considered literary appreciation, he had to fall back on the St George image: 'In an age when all good things were desperately assailed by tyrants, [when] so many at one time or another belittled the dangers on the one flank in order to concentrate on the dangers of the other, he almost alone from first to last dealt out his blows impartially and

Portrait of Orwell by Vernon Richards, 1945

defended without fear and without compromise the cause of liberty and the decencies from whatever quarter they might be assailed.'[381]

Orwell's reputation was sustained because, in the simplified, protracted Cold War environment of 'Good' versus 'Evil', literary 'quality' was a secondary consideration. George Woodcock labelled Orwell 'The Crystal Spirit' (a reference to the opening of *Homage to Catalonia*), explaining that 'those who knew Orwell have never been able to perform that act of faith demanded by so many modern critics, to see the writings isolated from the man. Always that gaunt, gentle, angry and endlessly controversial image intervenes, if only to remind one of how often his works were good talk turned into better prose.'[382] Richard Rees, in a short tribute, praised Orwell's 'kind of integrity and steadfastness' as being 'almost unique in his generation'.[383]

Once again, St George's 'decency' was held up in stark contrast to the enemy within: the English intelligentsia who wanted 'a breakdown of law and order which would produce a situation in Britain comparable to that in St Petersburg [Russia] in 1917'.[384] St George was 'a noble and colourful figure, large in act and vision, the almost complete opposite of the narrow-visioned academics who have closed in during the present generation on the literary worlds of both Britain and North America'.[385]

Until the late 1960s, there was little criticism to set against such adulation. A significant exception was a 1954 essay by Isaac Deutscher (named in Orwell's list of *suspects*) on *Nineteen Eighty-four*. Deutscher avoided mentioning the Crystal Spirit altogether and instead argued that the use of the novel was out of the author's hands: 'The novel has served as a sort of ideological super-weapon ... A book like *1984* may be used without much regard for the author's intention. Some of its features may be torn out of their context, while others, which do not suit the political purpose which the book is made to serve, are ignored or virtually suppressed.'[386]

Orwell's merit as a writer was tangential, or even distracting, for this was a case of a text being in the right Cold War place at the right Cold War time. 'Nor need a book like *1984* be a literary masterpiece or even an important and original work to make its impact,' Deutscher concluded. 'Indeed, a work of great literary merit is usually too rich in its texture and too subtle in thought and form to lend itself to adventitious exploitation. As a rule its symbols cannot easily be transformed into hypnotising bogies, or its ideas turned into slogans.'[387]

In 1968, Conor Cruise O'Brien (foreshadowing the debate over Orwell and the intelligence services that would take place 30 years later) used the revelation of CIA funding of intellectuals and authors to highlight the influence of Orwell ('a Tory eccentric with a taste for self-immolation') on imitators who were secretly sponsored by the US government.[388] Yet the image of Orwell as an icon of 'freedom' was strong enough to withstand the allegation.

An activist of the 'New Left' such as Noam Chomsky could still uphold Orwell as a model of the 'responsible intellectual'.[389]

It was Raymond Williams who extended the critique of Orwell in a series of books and essays in the 1970s. 'George Orwell' himself was a creation that served the interests of Eric Blair and, after his death, those with political and social agendas. Any activist, right or left, could hold up Orwell as a spokesman for their viewpoint, for Orwell was a 'paradox' and full of 'contradictions'. Behind this telling point, however, was the more fundamental objection: 'Orwell recognises and emphasises the complexity [of England], but he does not develop any kind of thinking which can sustain and extend a critical analysis of structures . . . Orwell hated what he saw of the consequences of capitalism, but he was never able to see it, fully, as an economic and political *system*.' The necessary outcome was his claim to a moral superiority. 'George Orwell' could only succeed through the 'successful impersonation of the plain man who bumps into experience in an unmediated way and is simply telling the truth about it'.[390]

Williams's formidable challenge to Orwell's hagiographers was written amid a tidal wave of new 'evidence' about him. In 1968, an edited collection of Orwell's essays and letters (selected by his widow Sonia Brownell and the curator of the Orwell Archive at University College, London) was published in four volumes. The BBC commemorated the 20th anniversary of Orwell's death, and books such as *The World of George Orwell* brought together memories of those who knew the man, descriptions of the environments – Burma, Paris, 1930s Britain, Spain – which shaped his writing, and assessments of his opinions.

The re-consecration of St George would come in the early 1980s with the juxtaposition of two events: the appearance of the most influential biography, Bernard Crick's *George Orwell: A Life*, and the approach of the year 1984. Crick's work made an impact because it

Orwell typing in his flat in Canonbury, winter 1945

was the first study based on Orwell's own papers, and also because Crick himself had a forceful political message to put across.

Crick tackled Williams by avoiding any confrontation with the argument that 'George Orwell' was a creation. Instead he erased the contradictions to resurrect the 'real' author, documented by his texts and correspondence, and to return him to the exalted simplicity of 'decency'. Orwell was a socialist, but he was an *English* socialist, a man concerned with morality rather than high intellect and theory: 'What was remarkable in Orwell was not his political position, which was common enough, but that he demanded publicly that his own side should live up to their principles, both in their lives and in their policies, should respect the liberty of others and tell the truth.'[391]

Crick and Williams both presented Orwell as a political rather than a literary figure. Crick claimed that some of Orwell's novels (notably *Coming Up for Air*) were underrated, but he was more concerned with Orwell as 'a supreme political writer', 'a great essayist' and 'a brilliant journalist'.[392] Similarly, the year 1984 became a convenient peg for the re-assertion of Orwell's political significance, cloaked in a moral superiority. As Robert Mulvihill asserted in a collection of essays based on one of the numerous Orwell conferences: 'Because of its underlying moral commitments and its identity of problems central to the democratic political experience, 1984 is a story for all seasons. The novel continues to provoke us to consider the substance of political decency and the threats to its survival.'[393]

Yet far from confirming the 'true' man and author, as Crick had attempted in his biography, the outpouring of comment in both popular and academic outlets highlighted the fact that 'George Orwell' was up for grabs. In a context where British and US politics had moved sharply to the right, he was claimed by neo-conservatives, free-marketeers, Cold War intellectuals, and a mass-market press trumpeting the wonders of Reaganism and Thatcherism. Norman Podhoretz, a leader of the anti-communist movement since the 1950s, titled his article for 1984, 'If Orwell were Alive Today, He'd be a Neo-Conservative'.[394] Margaret Thatcher attempted the difficult task of repudiating Orwell's pessimism while embracing him in freedom: 'George Orwell was wrong and . . . 1984 would be a year of hope and liberty.'[395] Rupert Murdoch's the *Sun*, the best-selling tabloid newspaper, followed suit:

> As 1984 opens, we have been spared the Orwell nightmare. We have liberty under Margaret Thatcher. We have hope of a better tomorrow.
>
> Yet all these things are not automatic.
>
> *We have to deserve them. We have to earn them.*

*We must be vigilant every day in 1984 and beyond to preserve them from any assault.*[396]

This interpretation was inevitably challenged by those with a stake in an Orwellian vision of a 'decent' left. Crispin Aubrey insisted that Orwell's 'unorthodox, libertarian position should appeal in fact to many on the current British left concerned for a broader, more humanitarian socialism.'[397] Crick maintained his appointment as Orwell's protector, writing numerous essays, advising the BBC on a three-part documentary, *Orwell Remembered*, and co-editing a book featuring the reminiscences of friends and acquaintances from Eric Blair's earliest days. Orwell's claim to the high moral ground, transcending any specific political and social argument, was projected in ever-loftier language. Orwell had 'a sensibility and perception that is close to observable experience and intensely practical', but was also 'a Pilgrim with his eyes raised towards Zion, head-in-the-air while feet necessarily tramp through the Slough of Despond and Vanity Fair'.[398] Others portrayed Orwell saving his readers, as in Patrick Reilly's assertion that 'prevention is Orwell's aim, and not simply because prevention is better than cure, but for the far more terrifyingly urgent reason that there must be prevention because there *is* no cure'.[399]

Yet, in one sense, this battle was a false one. Both the neo-conservatives and the 'decent' left had agreed upon an Orwell who was a model foe of the Soviet Union and its alleged sympathisers. Indeed it was a consensus that raised other problems, for the 'bad' left could turn that vigilance against the author. Conor Cruise O'Brien spoiled the eve of 1984 in the *Observer*: 'Anti-totalitarianism [as Orwell's aim] is misleading because it is not specific enough. *Nineteen Eighty-four* is not about some generalised form of oppression, which could be on the left and could be on the right. It is about . . . something which could only be communism as it developed in the Soviet Union. If [it] is even partially any kind of satire of our western way of life, I'm a Chinaman.'[400]

But Orwell's enemies had not gone away. A volume edited by Christopher Norris, *Inside the Myth: Orwell − Views from the Left*, extended Deutscher's 1954 allegation with the contention that 'Orwell has been kidnapped by the forces of reaction, taken over triumphantly by those who hold him up as *the* great example of a socialist who finally saw the light'; he had become 'the patron saint of current Cold-War doublethink'.[401] Some contributors went further by charging that Orwell was not the passive victim of the right but a collaborator with it, either through choice or the ambiguity of his writing.

The significance of the challenge, however, was that it was not limited to this narrow reading of the 'political'. Orwell was now being criticised for his attitudes towards and projections of the working class he supposedly championed and of the women who occupy an uncertain place in his writing. Beatrix Campbell brought the two aspects together when she sharply commented that Orwell not only ignored 'the culture of women, their concerns, their history, their movements', but made 'women the bearers of his own class hatred'. For Deidre Beddoe, Orwell, with 'some of the most obnoxious portrayals of women in English fiction . . . altered the record of the past, so far as women are concerned, as efficiently as if he had been in the employ of Minitrue. He was part of a conspiracy of silence.'[402] (Daphne Patai would subsequently develop a book-length argument, contending that 'manhood is the basic issue', in *The Orwell Mystique*.[403])

'George Orwell' survived this scrutiny if only because the 1950s portrayal of English decency was so well-established. Authors simply dismissed feminist quibbles, as in John Newsinger's remark that Patai was 'fundamentally wrong-headed'.[404] Conveniently, as Soviet communism collapsed, it could be casually observed that Orwell had been right all along. John Rodden used his book on the battle for Orwell's reputation to make his own sweeping claim that Orwell was 'a "true" intellectual . . . He flayed the left intelligentsia in order to fortify it, not to weaken it.'[405]

The elevation of the 'moral' author above any consideration of troublesome social and gender issues was best illustrated by the philosophers who led the fanfare for Orwell, albeit in emotive rather than philosophical terms. 'In the 40 years since Orwell wrote,' claimed Richard Rorty, 'nobody has come up with a better way of setting out the political alternatives which confront us.'[406] Michael Walzer was even more dramatic: 'The story of the last man was not intended to be his last word on politics. Nor need it be ours, so long as we speak with the terrifying awareness that was his gift.'[407]

Orwell's reputation was further buttressed by another wave of biographies. In 1991, Michael Shelden published *Orwell: The Authorised Biography* as a corrective to Crick, whom he claimed had reported Orwell's actions 'without commenting much on the motives and feelings behind them'.[408] The outcome was yet another narrative of the 'decent' man, peppered with assertions such as 'one of his remarkable qualities was his ability to face grim possibilities without losing all hope' and 'he was always analysing, always standing to one side and observing, trying to make sense of this life'.[409]

This process culminated in the mid-1990s, with Peter Davison's completion of a 20-year project to publish almost all of Orwell's writing. The 20 volumes added little that was not already known about the author, but the extensive press attention to their publication re-opened the debate on Orwell as a 'political' writer and personality. While Davison responded to the dismissal of Orwell as a 'literary' author, his primary mission was to re-confirm Orwell as the embodiment of the values of the 'liberal' society of the 20th century: 'Orwell's virtues are at their most attractive in his incredible determination to be a writer, whatever the difficulties and disappointments; in his passion for what he saw as social justice . . . to strive against the "beastly" for "decency" and, in writing to achieve that, to fight against the insistence of censors and publishers to "garble" what he said.' Davison even attempted to fashion an Orwell who would have relevance after the burial of the Soviet menace. Using the example of China, he invoked the ongoing fight against evil regimes and evil men who could suddenly appear, even at home: 'Were we able to hope that such regimes had no place in the modern world and that they would never arise in Britain, the "necessity" for *Nineteen Eighty-four* would disappear and the novel itself could become a footnote, a mere "problem in intellectual history". Until that happy and unlikely state occurs, it will remain an essential warning.'[410]

Davison's effort was just a bit too strident. Less than five years after the Soviet collapse, the revelations about Orwell's co-operation with the British intelligence services threatened to establish the author as a Cold War anachronism. Subsequent rescue efforts were telling for what they could not accomplish. Timothy Garton Ash tried to establish 'Orwell in Our Time' in May 2001 with the 'political' contention: 'The three dragons against which Orwell fought his good fight – European and especially British imperialism; fascism, whether Italian, German or Spanish; and communism, not to be confused with the democratic socialism in which Orwell himself believed – were all either dead or mortally weakened. Forty years after his own painful and early death, Orwell had won.'

Yet, for Orwell's contemporary relevance, Garton Ash had to fall back on a more prosaic notion: 'If I had to name a single quality that makes Orwell still essential reading in the 21st century, it would be his insight into the use and abuse of language.'[411] And so, in defending Orwell, the difficulty recurred: the emphasis on Orwell's 'political' and 'moral' qualities had been so protracted

Portrait of Orwell
by Peter Blake

that his resurrection as a literary figure – more than 60 years after Sean O'Casey had snapped that 'Orwell had as much chance of reaching the stature of Joyce as a tit has of reaching that of an eagle'[412] – seemed impossible.

Instead Orwell risked becoming a cultural cliché, used for every phenomenon from the prevalence of CCTV to so-called 'reality' television. For instance, in 2000 Jonathan Freedland, one of Britain's leading political columnists wrote: 'Just this once, believe the hype. *Big Brother* was billed as the summer's monster hit, and it is. Part gameshow, part docusoap, the Channel-4 programme has not just edged in front of BBC1 in the ratings. It has pulled off a trick thought possible only in television's golden past – creating a shared, collective experience. Sixteen years after 1984, Britain can declare: "Big Brother, we're watching you".'[413]

The safeguarding of Orwell's reputation would come not through his vigilance against the totalitarian threat but through the promotion of his 'Englishness'. As John Rossi wrote in 1992, 'Orwell never lost his faith in the rugged sense of the English people and their simple patriotism. They, and not the upper classes or the hopelessly degenerated intelligentsia, would save England.'[414] In an era where the political and economic development of Europe has forced a reassessment of British/English identity, Orwell was a comforting icon of superiority over continental Europe.[415] Jeffrey Meyers, in the culmination of more than 25 years examining the author, entitled his biography Orwell: Wintry Conscience of a Generation.[416]

And then the world changed once more on 11 September 2001. The attacks against the World Trade Center and the Pentagon revived the concept of a 'clash of civilisations', one in which there was no middle ground, no complexity of viewpoint. As President George W Bush warned: 'You're either with us or . . . with the terrorists.'[417] In this new Cold War, Orwell could once more be mobilised as the moral icon of the 'west', fending off the objections of deviant leftists; one only had to update his statement of 1947: The only big political questions in the world today are: for Russia – against Russia, for America – against America, for democracy – against democracy.[418]

All of these strands were woven together in Christopher Hitchens's 2002 tribute, Orwell's Victory (in the US, Why Orwell Matters). Like Orwell, Hitchens had framed himself as an honourable representative of the left who had become disillusioned with his comrades, especially after 11 September. Like Orwell, Hitchens had created an essential 'Englishness' which he was humbly promoting. And, just as Orwell tried to project himself through his praise of Charles Dickens, so Hitchens would use

Orwell to place himself as the leader of a 21st-century 'decency'.

In the end, however, Hitchens rescues for us an 'Orwell' who cannot engage with the issues of the 21st century because, now as well as then, he is beyond them: 'Politics are relatively unimportant, while principles have a way of enduring, as do the few irreducible individuals who maintain allegiance to them.'[419] The problem of what is to be done is replaced with the easier reassurance of who we 'are'.

# Conclusion: Escaping St George

Can we ever retrieve 'George Orwell'?

Of course, 'Orwell' will always be honoured. He is 'one of the inspiring political moralists of our age'.[420] He succeeded with 'his skill in rubbing the fur of his own cat backwards'.[421] 'Political writers should be the window cleaners of freedom [and] Orwell both tells and shows us how to do it . . . We need him still, because Orwell's work is never done.'[422]

Early in his career, Orwell had a sense of irony, even if it was no more than naming his dog Marx. He also recognised that the writer, for better or worse, is always being remade. He once wrote that the novelist John Galsworthy was *a bad writer, and some inner trouble, sharpening his sensitiveness, nearly made him into a good one; his discontent healed itself, and he reverted to type. It is worth pausing to wonder in just what form the thing is happening to oneself.*[423] The process was further complicated because *everyone in writing is torn between three motives; (i) Art for art's seeking(?) in the ivory tower, (ii) political propaganda, and (iii) pulling in the dough.*[424]

Even more importantly, Orwell realised that, in the end, there was no objective measurement of 'quality' in a writer. If the author remade himself in life, in death he was at the mercy of others: *In reality there is no kind of evidence or argument by which one can show that Shakespeare, or any other writer, is 'good' . . . Ultimately there is no test of literary merit except survival, which is itself an index to majority opinion.*'[425]

All this offered a caution against certainty: today's dogma could be tomorrow's folly. Instinctively, however, Orwell could not remain in a world of 'relative' judgements, for there were always evils to be fought, be it the menace of poverty, the threat of fascism, or the scourge of communism from Spain to the Cold War.

The difficulty for Orwell was that he had no answers for such challenges. Occasionally he acknowledged this, as in his admission of a lack of interest in economic and political theory or in the confession that he had produced *Trotskyist propaganda* in *Homage to Catalonia*, because *one's only experiences are being mixed up in contro-versies, intrigues, etc.*[426] More often, however, Orwell clung to the most general of platitudes. In 'Why I Write' (1946), he tried to sweep aside any relativism with the historical impulse for *true facts* and *political purpose*, but what he offered was little more than 'decency'. Once more, his elegy to Dickens offered a very uncomfortable recognition about Orwell himself: Dickens *had the most childish views of politics etc. but I think that, because his* moral *sense was sound, he would have been able to find his bearing in any political or economic milieu.*[427]

Decency was not enough in the world that Orwell observed, one in which *everyone* [was] *dishonest and . . . utterly heartless towards people who are outside the immediate range of his own interests and sym-pathies.*[428] If the common people were *at once too sane and too stupid to acquire the totalitarian outlook,*[429] they were also too sane and too stupid to bring about socialism. Orwell himself gave the game away in 1938: *What you get over and over again is a movement of the proletariat which is promptly canalised and betrayed by astute people at the top, and then the growth of a new governing class. The one thing that never arrives is equality. The mass of the people never get the chance to bring their innate decency into the control of affairs, so that one is almost driven to the cynical thought that men are only decent when they are powerless.*[430]

Orwell continued to insist that every line he wrote was *for* a democratic socialism that would empower the 'decent', but, lost for answers as to how this would come about, he usually preferred to strike out at would-be comrades. He was the honest crusader, warning the left: *Don't imagine that years on end you can make yourself the boot-licking propagandist of the Soviet regime, or any other regime, and then suddenly return to mental decency. Once a whore, always a whore.*[431] He was the sentinel of all writers who were *either pretending to be proletarians or indulging in public orgies of self-hatred because they were not proletarians.*[432] He could condemn *the present hunt after traitors and quislings* even as he damned the *quislings* supposedly allied with the Soviets, because he was honest where others were cunning.[433]

Orwell clung to this sense of 'decency', even when he accepted that he was *not a real novelist anyway;*[434] even when he admitted that there was not one day when *I did not feel that I was idling, that I was behind with the current job,* and *that my total output was miserably small.*[435] He died a valiant guardian against the totalitarianism of the future, but a guardian unable to offer any positive alternative to pessimism and fear.

One risks discomfort, even disillusionment, with this assessment of an icon. If not Orwell, then who would have led us through the Cold War, who will guide us in these times? Little wonder then that, despite reservations about Orwell's attitude towards women, towards 'natives', and even towards the working class, he continues to be upheld as a standard of 'decency'. As Orwell himself put it: *The fact to which we have got to cling, as a life-belt, is that it is possible to be a normal decent person and yet to be fully alive.*[436]

Because of Orwell's vagueness in his political philosophy, he can be stretched across a wide spectrum of political opinion. Bernard Crick can make the dubious assertion that Orwell is 'a libertarian, but of a specifically democratic socialist kind',[437] whereas Malcolm Muggeridge's Orwell is 'by temperament deeply conservative'.[438] In contrast, George Woodcock's Orwell is a 'radical dissenter'.[439]

In part, these alternative Orwells arose because Eric Blair could never close the gap between himself and the working class he supposedly championed. Woodcock realised this: 'Between the worker and the most radically minded of men there was a great gulf fixed and this gulf he never really crossed.'[440] Richard Hoggart observed that Orwell 'never quite lost the habit of seeing the working classes through the cosy fug of an Edwardian music-hall'.[441]

Perhaps this gap between Orwell and his subjects should not demote him from iconic status, but there is a further complication. Unable to provide a theoretical basis or a detailed programme for his politics, Orwell did not even choose to pursue the traditional foes of socialism and the working class. Instead, he turned on the 'left'. He defined his mission to Stephen Spender: *There are certain people like vegetarians and Communists whom one cannot answer. You just have to go on saying your say regardless of them, and then the extraordinary thing is that they may start listening.*[442]

Thus the same man who wrote of the *ever-present danger of becoming simply anti-Communist . . . which is completely sterile even if it isn't harmful,*[443] would take this risk in his writing from the 1930s to the end of his life. All the delicate nuances and complexities in his novels, particularly *Nineteen Eighty-four*, his support of 'freedom' in writing and in political activity, would be eclipsed by his animosity towards the left. Orwell might protest – when the tension between his 'positive' freedom and his 'negative' attacks came to the fore – that he was still a socialist, but he has left far too much unsaid for others to lay claim to after his death.

The list he passed to British intelligence services in 1949 might have had little effect – the IRD and MI6 had numerous other informers to help them compile their dossiers of 'good' and 'bad' writers, intellectuals and politicians – but it seriously undermines the saintly legacy of 'George Orwell'. The honourable dissenter was closing off the dissent of others with a note or query about their political beliefs, their ethnicity, and even their sexuality. The

contradictions within Orwell's definition of 'freedom' of thought and expression – and the liberalism he came to embody for many – were exposed. Orwell promoted 'freedom' as an objective standard, even as it was being denied to certain suspect individuals.

It is not George Orwell who needs to be rescued for us. We need to be rescued from 'Orwell'. Too often, the image has been preserved and promoted not to liberate thought but to contain it. 'Orwell' has been a useful crutch, a source of simple reassurance in the face of complex challenges. 'Orwell' has been used to define the 'acceptable' and the 'suspect' in theory and practice. And 'Orwell' has been used as a stick to beat those whose opinions are perceived as troublesome or in any way threatening.

The myth is simple; the reality is complex. In November 1945, Orwell wrote: *Whenever A and B are in opposition to one another, anyone who attacks or criticises A is accused of aiding and abetting B. And it is often, objectively and on a short-term analysis, that he is making things easier for B. Therefore say the supporters of A, shut up and don't criticise: or at least criticise 'constructively', which in practice always means favourably. And from this it is only a short step to arguing the suppression and distortion of known facts is the highest duty of a journalist.*[444]

Promoters of 'George Orwell' return again and again to this quotation as the highest example of his freedom of thought and expression by completing the analogy: because Orwell attacked or criticised the left, he was accused of aiding and abetting the enemy in the Second World War and capitalist schemers after the conflict. Yet what if Orwell's equation were completed as 'anyone who attacks or criticises anti-communist policy is accused of aiding and abetting the Soviet Union . . . Therefore say the supporters of anti-communist policy, shut up and don't criticise'? From this perspective, the people that Orwell accused of being 'suspect' from the 1930s to his death, the people that Orwell's anti-communist admirers regarded as dangerous, seem less like the enemy and more like victims of suppression and distortion. Orwell's decency is far from absolute.

Suddenly the Crystal Spirit isn't so crystal-clear. But perhaps, just perhaps, this element of uncertainty might be beneficial, allowing the doubters and the dissenters to emerge from under the shadow of 'George Orwell'.

*Geo. Orwell*

# Notes

1  Davison spent 20 years producing a 20-volume annotated collection of Orwell's writing, from his published texts to his correspondence to his secret notebooks.

2  George Orwell, *The Lion and the Unicorn: Socialism and the English Genius* (Harmondsworth: Penguin, 1982), p. 115.

3  George Orwell, 'The Prevention of Literature', *Polemic* (March 1946), in *The Collected Essays, Journalism & Letters of George Orwell* (hereafter *CEJL*),Volume 1 (London: Secker and Warburg, 1968), pp. 59–72.

4  The description of Barcelona in 1936 is in George Orwell, *Homage to Catalonia* (Harmondsworth: Penguin, 1966), pp. 8–10.

5  Michael Kelly, 'Phony Pacifists', *Washington Post* (3 October 2001), p. A31.

6  Christopher Hitchens, *Orwell's Victory* (London: Allen Lane, 2002), p. 3.

7  George Orwell, 'Why I Write', in *CEJL*,Volume 1 (London: Secker and Warburg, 1968), p. 1.

8  Michael Shelden, *Orwell: The Authorised Biography* (London: Minerva, 1992), p. 16, (hereafter Shelden).

9  'Why I Write', p. 1.

10 'Why I Write', p. 1.

11 Bernard Crick, *George Orwell: A Life* (Harmondsworth: Penguin, 1982), pp. 55–6 (hereafter Crick); Shelden, p. 23.

12 Shelden, p. 109.

13 George Orwell, 'Such, Such Were the Joys', *Partisan Review* (October–November 1952), in *CEJL*, Volume IV, p. 366.

14 *Partisan Review*, where the essay appeared in 1952, is an American journal.

15 Crick, p. 61.

16 Orwell to Connolly, 8 July 1938, in *CEJL*, Volume I, p. 343.

17 Anthony West, 'George Orwell', in *Principles and Persuasions* (Eyre & Spottiswoode, London, 1958).

18 Schoolmaster A. S. F. Gow, quoted in Crick, p. 105.

19 George Orwell, *The Road to Wigan Pier* (London: Penguin, 1962), p. 122.

20 George Orwell, 'The Sporting Spirit', *Tribune* (14 December 1945), in *CEJL*, Volume IV, pp. 40–4.

21 George Orwell, 'My Country, Right or Left', *Folios of New Writing*, Autumn 1940, in *CEJL*, Volume I, pp. 535–40.

22 See Crick, p. 109.

23 Poem written by Eric Blair on Burma government writing paper, undated, reprinted in Crick, pp. 161–2.

24 George Orwell, *The Road to Wigan Pier* (London: Penguin, 1962), p. 129.

25 Ruth Pitter quoted in 'Ruth Pitter's Personal Memories of George Orwell', British Broadcasting Corporation, January 1956, in Crick, pp. 178–80.

26 A 'spike' was a casual ward where homeless men could spend the night for a few pence.

27 Eric Blair, 'A Farthing Newspaper', *G.K.'s Weekly* (24 December 1928), in *CEJL*, Volume I, p. 12.

28 Rayner Heppenstall, *Four Absences* (London: Barrie and Rockcliff, 1960), p. 32.

29 Eric Blair, 'The Spike', *Adelphi* (April 1931), in *CEJL*, Volume I, pp. 36–43.

30 See Eric Blair, 'Hop-Picking', in *CEJL*, Volume I, pp. 52–71.

31 Eric Blair, 'A Hanging', *Adelphi* (August 1931), in *CEJL*, Volume I, pp. 44–8.

32 Blair to Collings, 12(?) October 1931, in *CEJL*, Volume I, p. 51.

33 Richard Rees, *George Orwell: Fugitive from the Camp of Victory* (London: Secker and Warburg, 1961), p. 143.

34 Eliot to Blair, 19 February 1932, quoted in Shelden, p. 167.

35  Mabel Fierz interview, October 1967, quoted in Shelden, p. 167.

36  Crick, pp. 214 and 223–4.

37  Blair to Moore, 26 April 1932, in CEJL, Volume I, pp. 77–8.

38  Blair to Moore, 19 November 1932, in CEJL, Volume I, p. 106.

39  Orwell to Heppenstall, 16 April 1940, in CEJL, Volume II, p. 22.

40  Times Literary Supplement (12 January 1933), p. 22; Cecil Day Lewis review, Adelphi (February 1933), pp. 381–2; J. B. Priestley review, Evening Standard (11 January 1933).

41  James Farrell review, New Republic (11 October 1933), pp. 256–7.

42  New Statesman review, quoted in Shelden, p. 182.

43  George Orwell, Down and Out in Paris and London (New York: Penguin, 1984), p. 5, (hereafter Down and Out).

44  Down and Out, p. 51.

45  Down and Out, p. 115.

46  Down and Out, p. 126.

47  Nicholas Shakespeare, 'Jilting Mr Blair', Daily Telegraph (16 September 1989), in Shelden, p. 145.

48  Crick, pp. 187–9.

49  Time and Tide (11 February 1933).

50  Introduction to 1935 French edition of Down and Out in Paris and London, in CEJL, Volume I, p. 115.

51  Quoted in Peter Stansky and William Abrahams, Orwell: The Transformation (London: Constable, 1979), pp. 23–4.

52  Manchester Guardian (9 January 1933).

53  There was the occasional 'political' article, such as 'Common Lodging Houses' in the New Statesman in September. Orwell castigated government legislation regulating social life, such as the separation of men and women, and concluded: It is absurd that [the unemployed] should be compelled to choose, as they are at present, between an easy-going pigsty and a hygienic prison. [CEJL, Volume I, pp. 97–100].

54  Orwell to Moore, 1 February 1933, in CEJL, Volume I, p. 115.

55  Orwell to Jaques, 18 February 1933, in Shelden, p. 189.

56  Orwell to Jaques, 25 May 1933, in CEJL, Volume I, p. 119.

57  Orwell to Moore, 26 November 1933,

58  See Cyril Connolly review in the New Statesman (6 July 1935).

59  Raymond Williams, Orwell (London: Fontana, 1971), p. 9.

60  Malcolm Muggeridge, 'A Knight of the Woeful Countenance', in Miriam Gross (ed), The World of George Orwell (London: Weidenfeld and Nicolson, 1971), p. 171.

61  Eric Blair, 'Comment on Exploite un Peuple: L'Empire Britannique en Birmanie', Le Progrès civique (4 May 1929).

62  Eric Blair, 'A Hanging', Adelphi (August 1931) , in CEJL, Volume I, pp. 44–8.

63  Introduction to Graham Holderness, Bryan Loughrey and Nahem Yousaf, George Orwell (Basingstoke: Macmillan, 1988), pp. 5–6.

64  George Orwell, 'Shooting an Elephant', New Writing (Autumn 1936), in CEJL, Volume I, pp. 235–41.

65  'Shooting an Elephant', p. 238.

66  Orwell diary, 3 April 1942, in CEJL, Volume II, p. 416.

67  Orwell diary, 10 April 1942, in CEJL, Volume II, p. 418.

68  George Orwell, 'On Kipling's Death', New English Weekly (23 January 1936), in CEJL, Volume I, p. 159.

69  George Orwell, 'Marrakech', New Writing (Christmas 1939), in CEJL, Volume I, p. 387.

70  George Orwell, 'Not Counting Niggers', Adelphi ( July 1939) in CEJL, Volume I, p. 394.

71  George Orwell, 'Rudyard Kipling', Horizon (February 1942), in CEJL, Volume II, pp. 184–96.

72  George Orwell, 'London Letter', Partisan Review (29 August 1942), in CEJL, Volume III, p. 232.

73  George Orwell, 'Reflections on Gandhi', Partisan Review ( January 1949), in CEJL, Volume IV, pp. 463–70.

74  Orwell to Salkeld, 27 July 1934, CEJL, Volume I, p. 136.

75  George Orwell, untitled poem, Adelphi (October 1933), in CEJL, Volume I, pp. 123–5.

76  George Orwell, A Clergyman's Daughter, in The Complete Novels (London: Penguin, 2000), pp. 385–9, hereafter cited as The Complete Novels.

in CEJL, Volume I, p. 125.

77 V. S. Pritchett review, *Spectator* (22 March 1935), p. 504; Peter Quennell review, *New Statesman and Nation* (23 March 1935), pp. 421–2; L. P. Hartley review, *Observer* (10 March 1935), p. 6.

78 Orwell to Salkeld, September 1934, in *CEJL*, Volume I, p. 139.

79 V. S. Pritchett review, *Spectator* (22 March 1935), p. 504.

80 Orwell to Moore, 3 October 1934, in *CEJL*, Volume I, p. 141.

81 Orwell to Moore, 14 November 1934, in *CEJL*, Volume I, p. 142.

82 Orwell to Salkeld, 16 February 1935, in *CEJL*, Volume I, p. 148.

83 George Orwell, *Keep the Aspidistra Flying*, in *The Complete Novels*, pp. 578–86.

84 *Keep the Aspidistra Flying*, in *The Complete Novels*, pp. 626–7.

85 Quoted in Crick, p. 254.

86 Orwell to Salkeld, 7 May 1935, in Shelden, p. 240.

87 Cyril Connolly review, *New Statesman and Nation* (25 April 1936), p. 635; Compton Mackenzie review, *Daily Mail*, cited in Peter Stansky and William Abrahams, *Orwell: The Transformation* (London: Constable, 1979), pp. 140–1.

88 Orwell to Woodcock, 28 September 1946, in *CEJL*, Volume IV, p. 22; 'Notes for a Literary Executor', quoted in Crick, p. 472.

89 Orwell to Salkeld, (August / September 1934?), in *CEJL*, Volume I, p. 138.

90 Orwell to Heppenstall, September(?) 1935, in *CEJL*, Volume I, p. 152.

91 Orwell to King-Farlow, 9 June 1936, in *CEJL*, Volume I, p. 224.

92 Rosalind Obermeyer (Orwell's landlady), quoted in Crick, p. 267.

93 George Orwell, *The Road to Wigan Pier* (Harmondsworth: Penguin, 1962), p. 18.

94 *The Road to Wigan Pier*, pp. 67–8.

95 Peter Stansky and William Abrahams, *Orwell: The Transformation* (London: Constable, 1979), p. 153.

96 Orwell to Common, 5 October 1936, in *CEJL*, Volume 1, p. 231.

97 Quoted in Sheila Hodges, *Gollancz: The Story of a Publishing House* (London: Gollancz, 1978), pp. 126–7.

98 *Road to Wigan Pier*, pp. 202–4.

99 *Road to Wigan Pier*, p. 130.

100 Harold Laski review, *Left News*, March 1937, pp. 275–6. Perhaps it is far from a trivial comment that Orwell reserved a special place for Laski in his criticism of intellectuals in the 1940s, focusing on Laski's writing style and never considering the substance of Laski's arguments.

101 Raymond Williams, *Orwell* (London: Fontana, 1971), p. 26.

102 Orwell to Collings, 16 August 1931, in *CEJL*, Volume I, p. 49. It was only on exceptional occasions that Orwell moved beyond reportage to evaluate a situation and make specific recommendations. One example was his September 1932 article in the *New Statesman* on 'Common Lodging Houses'. Orwell criticised council regulations, such as the spacing between beds, as being *in the nature of interference legislation – that is, they interfere, but not for the benefit of the lodgers*. [*CEJL*, Volume I, pp. 97–100].

103 Orwell diary, 31 January–25 March 1936, in *CEJL*, Volume I, pp. 170–214; *The Road to Wigan Pier*, pp. 11–2. The authenticity of Orwell's depiction has been challenged by local residents. 'In all my years around Wigan – I was a lad of 18 about the time that Orwell was going his rounds researching – I have never met, nor heard of anybody as filthy as the Brookers (the owners of the tripe shop in *The Road to Wigan Pier*). Dirt there was in plenty, but *filth* was something different. Unemptied chamberpots? All those I ever saw in those days were spotless. You had only to look over somebody's back yard, and they'd be lying there by the waste grid, emptied and washed.' [Former miner and Wigan resident John Farrimond, quoted in Peter Stansky and William Abrahams, *Orwell: The Transformation* (London: Constable, 1979), p. 150].

104 *The Road to Wigan Pier*, pp. 17, 21, 31 and 104.

105 Orwell diary, 19 February 1936, in *CEJL*, Volume 1, p. 181.

106 Even this example did not lead to further analysis but was fed into Orwell's crusade against socialism. Noting that the Liverpool Corporation was led by the Conservative Party rather than Labour and that the clearance was carried out by private contractors, Orwell concluded: *Beyond a certain point therefore, socialism and capitalism are not easy to distinguish, the state and the capitalist tend to merge into one.* [Orwell diary, 27 February 1936, in *CEJL*, Volume I, p. 189].

107 *The Road to Wigan Pier*, pp. 139, 149–152, 156 and 159; Orwell to Common, 5 October 1936, in *CEJL*, Volume I, p. 233.

108 *The Road to Wigan Pier*, pp. 185–6 and p. 193.

109 *The Road to Wigan Pier*, p. 199.

110 Orwell to Common, 16 (?) April 1936, in *CEJL*, Volume I, p. 216.

111 Orwell diary, 15 March 1936, in *CEJL*, Volume I, p. 203.

112 Gollancz to Rubinstein, 17 June 1932, reprinted in Crick, p. 224.

113 Orwell had doubted the book would be taken up by the LBC as it was *too fragmentary and, on the surface, not very left wing.* [Orwell to Moore, 15 December 1936, in *CEJL*, Volume I, p. 256].

114 Quoted in Shelden, p. 273.

115 Introduction to *The Road to Wigan Pier* (London: Gollancz, 1937), reprinted in Jeffrey Meyers, *George Orwell: The Critical Heritage* (London: Routledge and Kegan Paul, 1975), pp. 91–9.

116 Quoted in Crick, p. 310.

117 Orwell to Common, 19 February 1938, in *CEJL*, Volume I, p. 303.

118 George Orwell, *Homage to Catalonia* (Harmondsworth: Penguin, 1989), p. 189.

119 The Independent Labour Party had split from the better-known Labour Party after the latter, in the financial crisis of 1931, had carried out severe spending cuts and agreed to a coalition government with the Conservatives.

120 Hugh Thomas, *The Spanish Civil War* (Harmondsworth: Penguin, 1958), p. 946.

121 Orwell to Common, October (?) 1937,

in *CEJL*, Volume I, p. 289.

122 George Orwell, 'Spilling the Spanish Beans', *New English Weekly* (29 July and 2 September 1937), in *CEJL*, Volume I, pp. 269–76.

123 Orwell to Heppenstall, 31 July 1937, in *CEJL*, Volume I, p. 279.

124 See Edward Mendelson's *The English Auden* (Faber and Faber, London, 1977) for a history of 'Spain 1937'.

125 George Orwell, 'Inside the Whale', in *CEJL*, Volume I, p. 516.

126 Quoted in 'Divided They Stand: Writers on the Middle East Question', *The Independent* (9 October 2002).

127 George Orwell, review of Franz Borkenau's *The Spanish Cockpit* and John Summerfield's *Volunteer in Spain*, *Time and Tide* (31 July 1937), in *CEJL*, Volume I, pp. 276–8.

128 See, for example, George Orwell, review of Mary Low and Juan Brea's *Red Spanish Notebook* and R. Timmerman's *Heroes of Alcazar*, *Time and Tide* (9 October 1937), in *CEJL*, Volume I, pp. 287–8.

129 George Orwell, review of F. P. Crozier's *The Men I Killed*, *New Statesman* (28 August 1937), in *CEJL*, Volume I, pp. 282–3.

130 Desmond Flower review, *Observer*, 29 May 1938, quoted in Shelden, p. 320.

131 Quoted in John Atkins, *George Orwell* (London: John Calder, 1954), p. 51.

132 Geoffrey Gorer review, *Time and Tide* (30 April 1938), p. 599; John McNair, *New Leader* (6 May 1938), p. 7. Orwell joined McNair's Independent Labour Party weeks later.

133 Quoted in Crick, p. 364.

134 The same assessment was made in 1971 by Raymond Williams, who said *Homage to Catalonia* was 'in some ways Orwell's most important and most moving book' [Williams, p. 59].

135 *Homage to Catalonia*, p. 103.

136 *Homage to Catalonia*, p. 9.

137 *Homage to Catalonia*, pp. 16 and 28–9.

138 *Homage to Catalonia*, p. 7.

139 Orwell to Gollancz, 9 May 1937, in *CEJL*, Volume I, p. 267.

140 Orwell to Connolly, 8 June 1937, in *CEJL*, Volume I, p. 268.

141 Raymond Carr, 'Orwell and the Spanish Civil War', in Miriam Gross

(ed), *The World of George Orwell* (London: Weidenfeld and Nicolson, 1971), pp. 63–73.

142  Orwell to Jellinek, 20 December 1938, in *CEJL*, Volume I, p. 363.

143  Orwell to Spender, 2 April 1938, in *CEJL*, Volume I, p. 311.

144  George Orwell, 'As I Please', *Tribune* (4 February 1944), in *CEJL*, Volume II, p. 87.

145  Orwell letter to the editor of *New English Weekly* (26 May 1938), in *CEJL*, Volume 1, p. 332; Orwell to Spender, 2 April 1938, in *CEJL*, Volume 1, p. 313; *Homage to Catalonia*, pp. 64–5.

146  Orwell to Connolly, 27 April 1938, in *CEJL*, Volume I, p. 328.

147  George Orwell, review of Fenner Brockway's *Workers' Front*, *New English Weekly* (17 February 1938), in *CEJL*, Volume I, p. 304.

148  Orwell to Heppenstall, 31 July 1937, in *CEJL*, Volume I, p. 278.

149  George Orwell, 'Spilling the Spanish Beans', *New English Weekly* (29 July and 2 September 1937), in *CEJL*, Volume I, pp. 269–76.

150  George Orwell, 'Why I Joined the Independent Labour Party', *New Leader* (24 June 1938), in *CEJL*, Volume I, pp. 336–7.

151  George Orwell, 'Why I Joined the Independent Labour Party', *New Leader* (24 June 1938), in *CEJL*, Volume I, pp. 338.

152  Orwell to Read, 5 March 1939, in *CEJL*, Volume I, p. 387.

153  George Orwell, 'Not Counting Niggers', *Adelphi* (July 1939), in *CEJL*, Volume 1, p. 395.

154  Orwell to Read, 5 March 1939, in *CEJL*, Volume I, p. 387.

155  Orwell to Common, May (?) 1938, in *CEJL*, Volume I, p. 330.

156  George Orwell, 'In Defence of the Novel', *New English Weekly* (12–19 November 1936), in *CEJL*, Volume I, p. 249.

157  George Orwell, *Coming Up for Air*, in *The Complete Novels* (London: Penguin, 2000), p. 439.

158  *Coming Up for Air*, in *The Complete Novels*, p. 447.

159  *The Road to Wigan Pier*, p. 152.

160  *Coming Up for Air*, in *The Complete Novels*, pp. 559–60.

161  *Coming Up for Air*, in *The Complete Novels*, pp. 516–21.

162  *Coming Up for Air*, in *The Complete Novels*, pp. 521–5.

163  *Coming Up for Air*, in *The Complete Novels*, pp. 562 and 565.

164  *Coming Up for Air*, in *The Complete Novels*, p. 526.

165  George Orwell, 'Charles Dickens', in *Inside the Whale* (London: Victor Gollancz, 1940), in *CEJL*, Volume I, pp. 413–60.

166  'Charles Dickens', in *CEJL*, Volume I, pp. 457–8.

167  Q. D. Leavis, 'The Literary Life Respectable: Mr George Orwell', *Scrutiny* (September 1940), pp. 173–6.

168  George Orwell, review of Duchess of Atholl's *Searchlight on Spain*, *New English Weekly* (21 July 1938), in *CEJL*, Volume I, p. 344

169  George Orwell, 'Charles Reade', *New Statesman and Nation* (17 August 1940), in *CEJL*, Volume II, p. 34.

170  George Orwell, 'My Country Right or Left', *Folios of New Writing* (Autumn, 1940), in *CEJL*, Volume 1, p. 539.

171  George Orwell, *Tribune* (20 December 1940), quoted in Crick, p. 398.

172  George Orwell, 'London Letter', *Partisan Review* (March–April 1941), *CEJL*, Volume 2, pp. 49–55.

173  'Publisher's Announcement' of Searchlight Books, 1941, quoted in Crick, p. 402.

174  George Orwell, *The Lion and the Unicorn* (London: Penguin, 1982), pp. 104–10.

175  George Orwell diary, 18 April 1942, in *CEJL*, Volume II, p. 419.

176  *The Lion and the Unicorn*, p. 112.

177  *The Lion and the Unicorn*, pp. 37 and 41.

178  *The Lion and the Unicorn*, p. 37.

179  *The Lion and the Unicorn*, pp. 56–61.

180  *The Lion and the Unicorn*, pp. 40-1, 44, 48, 69, 73–80.

181  'The British Miracle', *Times Literary Supplement* (8 March 1941), p. 110.

182  George Orwell diary, 24 June 1940, in *CEJL*, Volume II, p. 354.

183  'My Country, Right or Left', pp. 535–40.

184  *The Lion and the Unicorn*, pp. 63–4.

185  George Orwell diary, 22 August

186 George Orwell, 'London Letter', *Partisan Review* (March–April 1942), p. 175.

187 George Orwell, review of Franz Borkenau, *The Totalitarian Enemy*, *Time and Tide* (4 May 1940), in *CEJL*, Volume II, p. 24.

188 George Orwell diary, 23 June 1941, in *CEJL*, Volume II, p. 405.

189 *The Lion and the Unicorn*, p. 93. Orwell would put forth shorter versions of his arguments in two essays written for the collection *Betrayal of the Left*, edited by Victor Gollancz, which came out at the same time as *The Lion and the Unicorn*. Two years later, he wrote the booklet *The English People*, with assertions such as *there is no revolutionary tradition in England, and even in extremist political parties, it is only the middle-class membership that thinks in revolutionary terms* and *the outstanding and – by contemporary standards – highly original quality is their habit of not killing one another*. Initially held up by problems with publication of the series in which it was to appear, *The English People* finally appeared in 1947 as Britain was deciding its political position in the emerging Cold War. [George Orwell, *The English People* (London: Collins, 1947), reprinted in *CEJL*, Volume III, pp. 3 and 30].

190 Orwell to Gollancz, 8 January 1940, in *CEJL*, Volume I, p. 409.

191 George Orwell diary, 25 October 1940, in *CEJL*, Volume II, p. 377.

192 George Orwell diary, 15 April 1941, in *CEJL*, Volume II, p. 395.

193 Orwell to Common, 20 April 1938, in *CEJL*, Volume II, p. 314

194 Orwell to Lehmann, 6 July 1940, in *CEJL*, Volume II, p. 29.

195 George Orwell, letter to the editor of *Time and Tide*, 22 June 1940, in *CEJL*, Volume II, p. 278.

196 See Crick, p. 382.

197 George Orwell, review of *The Great Dictator*, *Time and Tide* (21 December 1940), summarised in Shelden, pp. 353–4

198 Malcolm Muggeridge, *Chronicles of Wasted Time*, Volume II (London: Collins, 1978), p. 73.

199 George Orwell diary, 23 July 1942, in *CEJL*, Volume II, p. 437.

200 Alex Comfort and George Woodcock contributions, 'A Controversy', *Partisan Review* (September–October 1942), *CEJL*, Volume II, pp. 223–6.

201 George Orwell contribution, 'A Controversy', *Partisan Review* (September-October 1942), *CEJL*, Volume II, pp. 227–30.

202 George Orwell, 'London Letter', *Partisan Review* (July-August 1942), *CEJL*, Volume II, pp. 207–16.

203 George Orwell diary, 21 June 1942, in *CEJL*, Volume II, p. 432.

204 Orwell to Woodcock, 2 December 1942, in *CEJL*, Volume II, p. 267; Orwell to Comfort, 11 (?) July 1943, in *CEJL*, Volume II, p. 303.

205 Orwell to Heppenstall, 24 August 1943, in *CEJL*, Volume II, p. 305.

206 George Orwell, 'London Letter', *Partisan Review* (March–April 1943), in *CEJL*, Volume III, p. 276.

207 George Orwell, 'Literature and the Left', *Tribune* (4 June 1943), in *CEJL*, Volume II, pp. 292–4.

208 George Orwell, review of Lionel Fielden's *Beggar My Neighbour*, *Horizon* (September 1943), in *CEJL*, Volume II, p. 306.

209 'London Letter', *Partisan Review* (Winter 1945), in *CEJL*, Volume III, p. 294.

210 Quoted in Crick, p. 445.

211 Michael Foot, 'Obituary for Aneurin Bevan', *Tribune* (8 July 1960).

212 T. R. Fyvel, 'The Years at Tribune' in Miriam Gross (ed.), *The World of George Orwell* (London: Weidenfeld and Nicolson, 1971), pp. 113–4.

213 George Orwell, 'Boys' Weeklies', *Horizon* (March 1940), in *CEJL*, Volume I, p. 460–93.

214 George Orwell, 'The Art of Donald McGill', *Horizon* (September 1941), in *CEJL*, Volume II, pp. 155–65.

215 George Orwell, 'Benefit of Clergy: Some Notes on Salvador Dali', June 1944, in *CEJL*, Volume III, pp. 156–65.

216 George Orwell, 'Raffles and Miss Blandish', *Horizon* (October 1944) and *Politics* (November 1944), in *CEJL*, Volume III, pp. 212–24.

217 George Orwell, review of Edward Blunden's *Cricket Country*, *Manchester Evening News* (20 April 1944), in *CEJL*,

Volume III, pp. 47–50.

218 George Orwell, 'Some Thoughts on the Common Toad', *Tribune*, 12 April 1946, in *CEJL*, Volume IV, pp. 141–5.

219 George Orwell, 'A Nice Cup of Tea', *Evening Standard*, 12 January 1946, in *CEJL*, Volume III, p. 40.

220 George Orwell, 'As I Please', *Tribune* (24 December 1943), in *CEJL*, Volume III, pp. 63–5.

221 George Orwell, 'As I Please', *Tribune* (18 August 1944), in *CEJL*, Volume III, p. 207; George Orwell, 'As I Please', *Tribune* (6 October 1944), in *CEJL*, Volume III, p. 248.

222 A rare exception was a column in the *Observer* in April 1944 which considered the contrasting 'capitalist' thought of the political and economic philosopher Friedrich von Hayek and the 'collectivist' thought of Konni Zilliacus, a left-wing Labour Member of Parliament. [George Orwell, review of Friedrich von Hayek's *The Road to Serfdom* and Konni Zilliacus's *The Mirror of the Past*, *Observer* (9 April 1944), in *CEJL*, Volume III, pp. 117–9].

223 George Orwell, 'As I Please', *Tribune* (28 July 1944), in *CEJL*, Volume III, pp. 197–9.

224 George Orwell, 'As I Please', *Tribune* (2 February 1945), in *CEJL*, Volume III, pp. 326–9.

225 George Orwell, 'As I Please', *Tribune* (11 February 1944), in *CEJL*, Volume III, pp. 89–93.

226 George Orwell, 'As I Please', *Tribune* (8 December 1944), in *CEJL*, Volume III, pp. 288–91.

227 George Orwell, 'As I Please', *Tribune* (8 September 1944) in *CEJL*, Volume III, pp. 228–31.

228 Crick, p. 263; George Orwell, review of Sean O'Casey's *Drums under the Windows*, *Observer* (28 October 1945), in *CEJL*, Volume IV, pp. 13–15; George Orwell, 'As I Please', *Tribune* (14 February 1947), in *CEJL*, Volume IV, pp. 284–5.

229 George Orwell, *The English People* (London: Collins, 1947), in *CEJL*, Volume III, p. 38.

230 George Orwell, 'London Letter', *Partisan Review* (Summer 1944), in *CEJL*, Volume III, pp. 123–8.

231 George Orwell, 'London Letter', *Partisan Review* (Winter 1945), in *CEJL*, Volume III, pp. 293–9.

232 George Orwell, 'London Letter', *Partisan Review* (Spring 1944), in *CEJL*, Volume III, p. 74.

233 George Orwell, 'London Letter', *Partisan Review* (Fall 1944), in *CEJL*, Volume III, p. 191.

234 George Orwell, 'London Letter', *Partisan Review* (Summer 1945), in *CEJL*, Volume III, pp. 380–6.

235 George Orwell diary, 19 May 1942, in *CEJL*, Volume II, p. 426; see Crick, p. 481.

236 George Orwell, 'London Letter', *Partisan Review* (Fall 1945), in *CEJL*, Volume III, pp. 393–400.

237 George Woodcock, *The Crystal Spirit: A Story of George Orwell* (London: Jonathan Cape, 1967), p. 28.

238 George Orwell, review of Bertrand Russell's *Power: A New Social Analysis*, *Adelphi* (January 1939), pp. 375–7.

239 George Orwell, 'New Words', unpublished, 1940?, in *CEJL*, Volume II, pp. 3–12.

240 George Orwell; 'Literature and Totalitarianism', *Listener* (19 June 1941), in *CEJL*, Volume II, p. 137.

241 George Orwell, 'London Letter', *Partisan Review* (July–August 1941), in *CEJL*, Volume II, pp. 112–22; George Orwell, 'Wells, Hitler, and the World State', *Horizon* (August 1941), in *CEJL*, Volume II, pp. 139–45.

242 George Orwell, 'Literature and the Left', *Tribune* (4 June 1943), in *CEJL*, Volume II, pp. 292–4.

243 George Orwell, 'Arthur Koestler', *Focus* (1946), in *CEJL*, Volume III, pp. 234–44.

244 See Orwell's discussion of Walter Raleigh and his aborted *History of the World* in 'As I Please', *Tribune* in *CEJL*, Volume III, pp. 87–9.

245 George Orwell, 'As I Please', *Tribune* (2 June 1944), in *CEJL*, Volume III, pp. 165–8.

246 George Orwell, 'As I Please', *Tribune* (17 March 1944), in *CEJL*, Volume III, pp. 109–11.

247 George Orwell, 'As I Please', *Tribune* (4 February 1944), in *CEJL*, Volume III, pp. 87–9.

248 George Orwell, 'As I Please', *Tribune*

(13 October 1944), in *CEJL*, Volume III, Ibid., p. 252–5.

249  George Orwell, 'London Letter', *Partisan Review* (Summer 1944), in *CEJL*, Volume III, pp. 123–8; Orwell to Willmett, 18 May 1944, in *CEJL*, Volume III, p. 149.

250  From the 'Preface' to the Ukrainian edition of *Animal Farm*, 1947, reprinted in *CEJL*, Volume III, pp. 405–6.

251  Orwell to Struve, 17 February 1944, in *CEJL*, Volume III, p. 95.

252  George Orwell, 'Why I Write', in *CEJL*, Volume I, p. 7.

253  Quoted in Crick, p. 454.

254  Cape added insult to injury with the suggestion that the manuscript 'would be less offensive if the predominant caste in the fable were not pigs. I think the choice of pigs as the ruling caste will no doubt give offence to many people, and particularly to anyone who is a bit touchy, as undoubtedly the Russians.' [Orwell to Moore, 19 June 1944, reprinted in Crick, p. 456].

255  Eliot to Orwell, 13 July 1944, quoted in Crick, pp. 437–8.

256  Orwell to Moore, 23 January 1946, in *CEJL*, Volume IV, p. 110.

257  George Orwell, *Animal Farm*, in *The Complete Novels* (London: Penguin, 2000), pp. 14–16 and 66.

258  Stephen Sedley, 'An Immodest Proposal: *Animal Farm*', in Christopher Norris (ed.), *Inside the Myth – Orwell: Views from the Left* (London: Fontana, 1984), p. 159.

259  Quoted in W Averell Harriman and Elie Abel, *Special Envoy to Churchill and Stalin, 1941–6* (New York: Random House, 1975), p. 283.

260  George Orwell, review of S. Casado's *The Last Days of Madrid*, *Time and Tide* (20 January 1940), in *CEJL*, Volume I, p. 411.

261  George Orwell, 'London Letter', *Partisan Review* (July–August 1943), in *CEJL*, Volume II, p. 286; Orwell to Murry, 5 August 1944, in *CEJL*, Volume III, p. 202.

262  Orwell to Macdonald, 5 December 1946, quoted in Shelden, p. 407.

263  George Orwell, 'London Letter', *Partisan Review* (Summer 1945), in *CEJL*, Volume III, p. 380.

264  Kingsley Martin review, *New Statesman and Nation*, 8 September 1945, p. 166.

265  See Crick, pp. 488–9.

266  Orwell to Moore, 23 February 1946, in *CEJL*, Volume IV, p. 109.

267  George Orwell, 'As I Please', *Tribune*, 3 December 1943, in *CEJL*, Volume III.

268  George Orwell, 'Riding Down from Bangor', *Tribune*, 22 November 1946, in *CEJL*, Volume IV, pp. 242–7.

269  George Orwell, review of Lewis Mumord's *Herman Melville*, *New Adelphi* (March–May 1930), in *CEJL*, Volume I, pp. 19–22.

270  George Orwell, 'Notes on Nationalism', *Polemic* (October 1945), in *CEJL*, Volume III, pp. 361–80.

271  George Orwell, 'The Prevention of Literature', *Polemic* (March 1946), in *CEJL*, Volume IV, pp. 59–72.

272  George Orwell, 'Politics and the English Language', *Horizon* (April 1946), in *CEJL*, Volume IV, pp. 127–40. It should be noted, for some balance, that Orwell did broaden his scope in this case to consider, as examples of political language as *the defence of the indefensible*, support for continued British rule in India and the dropping of the atomic bomb on Japan, and he emphasised that the effort *to make lies sound truthful and murder respectable* can be true of *all political parties, from Conservatives to Anarchists*.

273  George Orwell, editorial for *Polemic* (May 1946), in *CEJL*, Volume IV, pp. 153–60.

274  George Orwell, 'Politics v. Literature: An Examination of *Gulliver's Travels*', *Polemic* (September-October 1946), in *CEJL*, Volume IV, pp. 205–23.

275  George Orwell, 'Second Thoughts on James Burnham', *Polemic* (May 1946), in *CEJL*, Volume IV, pp. 160–81.

276  George Orwell, 'Why I Write', in *CEJL*, Volume I, pp. 1–7.

277  Orwell to Rahv, 14 October 1943, in *CEJL*, Volume II, p. 317.

278  David Cesarani, *Arthur Koestler: The Homeless Mind* (London: William Heinemann, 1998), pp. 305–10.

279  George Orwell, 'Arthur Koestler', *Focus* (1946), in *CEJL*, Volume III,

pp. 234–44; George Orwell, 'Catastrophic Gradualism', *Commonwealth Review* (November 1945) and *Politics* (September 1946), in *CEJL*, Volume IV, p. 15.

280 Orwell diary, 26 January 1941, in *CEJL*, Volume II, p. 381; Orwell diary, 10 January 1943, in *CEJL*, Volume II, p. 447.

281 George Orwell, 'As I Please', *Tribune* (17 January 1947), in *CEJL*, Volume IV, p. 268.

282 George Orwell, 'Freedom of the Park', *Tribune* (7 December 1945), in *CEJL*, Volume IV, p. 37.

283 George Orwell, 'As I Please', *Tribune* (26 January 1945), in *CEJL*, Volume III, p. 323.

284 Quoted in Irving Howe, 'Orwell and America', in Rob Kroes (ed.), *Nineteen Eighty-four and the Apocalyptic Imagination in America* (Amsterdam: Free University Press, 1985), p. 28.

285 George Orwell, 'London Letter', *Partisan Review* (Summer 1946), in *CEJL*, Volume IV, pp. 184–91.

286 Arthur Schlesinger, Jr., 'The U.S. Communist Party', *Life* (July 1946), p. 84.

287 George Orwell to Fredric Warburg, 31 May 1947, in *CEJL*, Volume IV, p. 329.

288 Quoted in Francis Hope, 'Schooldays', in Miriam Gross (ed.), *The World of George Orwell* (London: Weidenfeld and Nicolson, 1971), p. 17.

289 Orwell to Warburg, 4 February 1948, in *CEJL*, Volume IV, p. 404.

290 Orwell to Warburg, 21 December 1948, in *CEJL*, Volume IV, p. 459.

291 Orwell to Warburg, 22 October 1948 and 21 December 1948, in *CEJL*, Volume IV, pp. 448 and 459.

292 Orwell to Warburg, 31 May 1947, in *CEJL*, Volume IV, p. 329.

293 George Orwell, 'Pleasure Spots', *Tribune*, 11 January 1946, in *CEJL*, Volume IV, pp. 78–82.

294 George Orwell, 'Raffles and Miss Blandish', *Horizon* (October 1944), in *CEJL*, Volume III, p. 222.

295 George Orwell, *Nineteen Eighty-four*, in *The Collected Novels* (London: Penguin, 2000), p. 892.

296 Veronica Wedgwood, *Time and Tide*, 11 June 1949, pp. 494–5.

297 V. S. Pritchett, *New Statesman and Nation*, 18 June 1949, pp. 646–8; Julian Symons review, *Times Literary Supplement*, 10 June 1949, p. 380.

298 Diana Trilling review, *Nation*, 25 June 1949, p. 716.

299 *Nineteen Eighty-four*, in *The Collected Novels*, p. 773.

300 *Nineteen Eighty-four*, in *The Complete Novels*, p. 762.

301 *Nineteen Eighty-four*, in *The Complete Novels*, p. 821.

302 *Nineteen Eighty-four*, in *The Complete Novels*, p. 751.

303 There is also the literal whore in the text, the degraded prostitute whose cardboard mask finally yields to *a cavernous blackness* and the face of *quite an old woman, fifty years old at least.* [*Nineteen Eighty-four*, in *The Complete Novels*, p. 783]

304 *Nineteen Eighty-four*, in *The Complete Novels*, pp. 748, 817 and 868.

305 *Nineteen Eighty-four*, in *The Complete Novels*, p. 825.

306 *Nineteen Eighty-four*, in *The Complete Novels*, p. 867.

307 'The Truman Doctrine', speech to Congress, 12 March 1947, quoted in Scott Lucas, *Freedom's War: The US Crusade against the Soviet Union, 1945–1956* (New York: New York University Press, 1999), pp. 6–7.

308 Quoted in Irwin Ross, *The Loneliest Campaign* (New York: New American Library, 1968), pp. 23–4.

309 See W. Scott Lucas and C. J. Morris, 'A Very British Crusade: the Information Research Department and the Beginning of the Cold War,' in Richard Aldrich (ed.), *British Intelligence, Strategy, and the Cold War* (London: Routledge, 1992), pp. 85–110.

310 Orwell to Henson, 16 June 1949, in *CEJL*, Volume IV, p. 502.

311 Quoted in Les K. Adler and Thomas G. Paterson, 'Red Fascism: The Merger of Nazi Germany and Soviet Russia in the American Image of Totalitarianism, 1930s–1950s,' *American Historical Review* (April 1970), pp. 1046–64.

312 For an introduction to the Frankfurt School, see Martin Jay, *The Dialectical Imagination: A History of the Frankfurt*

School and the Institute of Social Research 1923–1950 (Berkeley: University of California Press, 1996).

313 George Orwell, 'As I Please', Tribune (22 November 1946), in CEJL, Volume IV, p. 247.

314 George Orwell, 'You and the Atom Bomb', Tribune (19 October 1945), in CEJL, Volume IV, pp. 6–10.

315 Fredric Warburg, 'Publisher's Report', December 1948, in Jeffrey Meyers, George Orwell: The Critical Heritage (London: Routledge and Kegan Paul, 1975), p. 247.

316 Isaac Deutscher, '1984 – The Mysticism of Cruelty', in Russia in Transition and Other Essays (London: Hamish Hamilton, 1957), p.245.

317 David Hencke and Rob Evans, 'How Big Brother Used Orwell to Fight the Cold War', Guardian (30 June 2000).

318 New York Times, 12 June 1949.

319 Philip Rahv, Partisan Review (July 1949) in Jeffrey Meyers, George Orwell: The Critical Heritage (London: Routledge and Kegan Paul, 1975), p. 267.

320 Orwell to Henson, 16 June 1949, in CEJL, Volume IV, p. 502.

321 Warburg memorandum, 1948, in Crick, p. 567.

322 Howe in Kroes (ed.), p. 30.

323 Nineteen Eighty-four, in The Complete Novels, p. 783.

324 Nineteen Eighty-four, in The Complete Novels, p. 784; Mark Crispin Miller quoted in Rob Kroes, 'A Nineteen Eighty-Foreboding: Orwell and the Entropy of Politics', in Kroes (ed.), p. 86.

325 Nineteen Eighty-four, in The Complete Novels, p. 797.

326 Richard Rees, George Orwell: Fugitive from the Camp of Victory (London: Secker and Warburg, 1961), p. 88.

327 Beatrix Campbell, 'Orwell – Paterfamilias or Big Brother?', in Norris (ed.), p. 135.

328 Peter Davison, The Complete Works of George Orwell, Volume XX, Our Job is to Make Life Worth Living (London: Secker and Warburg, 1998), p. 318. Celia Kirwan, later Goodman, died in October 2002. See the obituary in The Independent, 25 October 2002.

329 See Lucas, W. S. and Morris, C. J. 'A Very British Crusade: The Information Research Department and the Beginning of the Cold War' in Richard Aldrich (ed.), British Intelligence, Strategy, and the Cold War (London: Routledge, 1992); Lashmur, Paul and Oliver, James, Britain's Secret Propaganda War (Stroud: Sutton, 1998).

330 Quoted in Davison, The Complete Works, p. 319.

331 Davison, The Complete Works, p. 240.

332 Peter Davison, the editor of 20 volumes of Orwell's correspondence and writings, has published an abridged version with 28 names deleted. The notations besides those names which are 'open' are taken from Davison, The Complete Works, pp. 242–58.

333 The 1941 Time and Tide review of Chaplin is quoted in Shelden, p. 354.

334 George Orwell, review of J. B. Priestley's Angel Pavement, Adelphi (October 1930), p. 25.

335 Schlesinger, 'The U.S. Communist Party', Life (July 1946) p. 88.

336 Davison, The Complete Works, p. 319.

337 Quoted in Davison, The Complete Works, p. 320.

338 Quoted in Davison, The Complete Works, p. 323.

339 Orwell to Kirwan, 6 April 1949, in Davison, The Complete Works, pp. 322–3.

340 See Frank Johnson, 'Orwell was right to spy for Britain', Daily Telegraphy (12 July 1996); Bernard Crick, 'Blair vs. the Left', Guardian (12 July 1996); Mervyn Jones, 'Fears that made Orwell sneak on his friends', Guardian (13 July 1996); Geoffrey Wheatcroft, Independent on Sunday (28 June 1998); Christopher Hitchens letters, London Review of Books (6 January and 3 February 2000); Timothy Garton Ash, 'Orwell for our Time', Guardian (5 May 2001).

341 Orwell to Rees, 3 March 1949, in CEJL, Volume IV, p. 478.

342 Orwell to Richards, 6 August 1946, in CEJL, Volume IV, p. 197.

343 George Orwell, 'Burnham's View of the Contemporary World Struggle', New Leader (29 March 1947) in CEJL, Volume IV, p. 313.

344 George Orwell, 'Burnham's View of the Contemporary World Struggle',

*New Leader* (29 March 1947) in *CEJL*, Volume IV, p. 313.

345 Orwell to Woodcock, 23 March 1948, in *CEJL*, Volume IV, p. 414.

346 Orwell to Koestler, 20 September 1947, in *CEJL*, Volume IV, p. 379.

347 Orwell to Symons, 21 March 1948, in *CEJL*, Volume IV, p. 406.

348 Orwell to Woodcock, 4 January 1948, in *CEJL*, Volume IV, p. 401.

349 Konni Zilliacus and George Orwell letters to *Tribune* (17 January 1947), in *CEJL*, Volume IV, pp. 191–4.

350 Orwell to Symons, 29 October 1948, in *CEJL*, Volume 4, pp. 449–51.

351 George Orwell, 'Writers and Leviathan', *Politics and Letters* (Summer 1948) and *New Leader* (19 June 1948), in *CEJL*, Volume IV, pp. 407–14.

352 George Orwell, 'Toward European Unity', *Partisan Review* (July-August 1947), in *CEJL*, Volume IV, pp. 370–5.

353 Quoted in Lucas and Morris, pp. 94–5.

354 John Newsinger, *Orwell's Politics* (Basingstoke: Macmillan, 1999), p. 136.

355 George Orwell, 'Britain's Struggle for Survival: The Labor Government After Three Years', *Commentary* (October 1948), pp. 343–9.

356 Orwell to Fyvel, 15 April 1949, in *CEJL*, Volume IV, p. 492.

357 Orwell to Fyvel, 31 December 1947, in *CEJL*, Volume IV, p. 386.

358 George Orwell, review of Oscar Wilde's *The Soul of Man under Socialism*, *Observer* (9 May 1948), in *CEJL*, Volume IV, p. 426.

359 T. R. Fyvel, 'A Writer's Life', *World Review* (June 1950), p. 18.

360 C. M. Woodhouse, 'Animal Farm', *Times Literary Supplement* (6 August 1945), pp. xxx-xxxi.

361 Woodhouse was one of the key MI6 personnel involved in the planning and execution of the 1953 overthrow of the Mossadegh government in Iran, which had offended Britain with the nationalisation of the Anglo-Iranian Oil Company. [See C. M. Woodhouse, *Something Ventured* (London: Granada, 1982)]

362 See Frances Stonor Saunders, *Who Paid the Piper? The CIA and the Cultural Cold War* (London: Granta, 1999), p. 300.

363 David Hencke and Rob Evans, 'How Big Brother Used Orwell to Fight the Cold War', *The Guardian*, 30 June 2000.

364 Richard Norton-Taylor and Seamus Milne, *Guardian*, 11 July 1996, p. 1; Scott Lucas, *Freedom's War: The US Crusade Against the Soviet Union 1945–56* (New York: New York University Press, 1999), pp. 64–5; Frances Stonor Saunders, *Who Paid the Piper? The CIA and the Cultural Cold War* (London: Granta, 1999), pp. 293–301.

365 Quoted in Irving Howe, 'Orwell and America', in Rob Kroes (ed.), *Nineteen Eighty-four and the Apocalyptic Imagination in America* (Amsterdam: Free University Press, 1985), p. 28.

366 Alan Brown, 'Examining Orwell: Political and Literary Values in Education', in Christopher Norris (ed.), *Inside the Myth – Orwell: Views from the Left* (London: Fontana, 1984), p. 40.

367 Stephen Spender, *World Review* (June 1950), p. 51.

368 Tom Hopkinson, *World Review* (June 1950), quoted in Crick, p. 490.

369 Julian Symons, 'Tribune's Obituary', reprinted in Audrey Coppard and Bernard Crick (eds.), *Orwell Remembered* (London: Ariel, 1984), p. 275.

370 Koestler and Pritchett quoted in David Pryce-Jones, 'Orwell's Reputation', in Miriam Gross (ed.), *The World of George Orwell* (London: Weidenfeld and Nicolson, 1971), p. 150.

371 Lionel Trilling, 'George Orwell and the Politics of Truth', in *The Opposing Self* (London: Secker and Warburg, 1955), p. 371.

372 Obituary of George Orwell, 'Criticism and Allegory', *The Times*, 23 January 1950, p. 7.

373 John Atkins, *George Orwell* (London: Calder and Boyars, 1945), p. 1.

374 George Woodcock, 'Reflections of George Orwell', *Northern Review* (August/September 1953), in Audrey Coppard and Bernard Crick (eds.), *Orwell Remembered* (London: Ariel,

1984), pp. 199–234; Richard Peters interview, 9 September 1955, British Broadcasting Corporation, in Coppard and Crick (eds.), p. 90.

375  Quoted in Crick, p. 638.

376  A. L. Morton, *The English Utopia* (London: Laurence and Wishart, 1952), quoted in Crispin Aubrey, 'The Making of 1984', in Crispin Aubrey and Paul Chilton (eds.), *Nineteen Eighty-four in 1984: Autonomy, Control, and Communication* (London: Comedia, 1983), p. 11.

377  George Mayberry review, *New Republic*, 23 June 1952, p. 22; Herbert Matthews, *Nation*, 27 December 1952, p. 597

378  Irving Howe, 'Orwell: History as Nightmare', *American Scholar* (Spring 1956), reprinted in *Politics and the Novel* (London: Stevens and Sons, 1961), p. 236.

379  John Wain review, *Twentieth Century* (January 1954), p. 71.

380  Stephen Spender interview, 7 May 1963, reprinted in Coppard and Crick (eds.), p. 262; Anthony Powell, 'George Orwell: A Memoir', *Atlantic Monthly* (October 1967), reprinted in Coppard and Crick (eds.), p. 247.

381  Christopher Hollis, *A Study of George Orwell: The Man and His Works* (London: Hollis and Carter, 1956), p. 208.

382  George Woodcock, *The Crystal Spirit* (London: Jonathan Cape, 1967), p. 7.

383  Richard Rees, *George Orwell: Fugitive from the Camp of Victory* (London: Secker and Warburg, 1961), p. 12.

384  Rees, p. 45.

385  Woodcock, p. 7.

386  Deutscher, '1984 – The Mysticism of Cruelty', in *Russia in Transition and Other Essays* (London: Hamish Hamilton, 1957), p. 230.

387  Deutscher, p. 231.

388  Conor Cruise O'Brien, *Listener* (12 December 1968), pp. 797–8.

389  See the discussion of the Spanish Civil War in Noam Chomsky, 'Objectivity and Liberal Scholarship' in *American Power and the New Mandarins*, (London: Chatto and Windus, 1969) pp. 65–98.

390  Raymond Williams, *Orwell* (London: Fontana, 1971), pp. 23 and 26.

391  Crick, pp. 17–8.

392  Crick, pp. 18–20.

393  Robert Mulvihill (ed.), *Reflections on America, 1984: An Orwell Symposium* (Athens: University of Georgia Press, 1986), p. 1.

394  Norman Podhoretz, 'If Orwell were Alive Today, He'd be a Neo-Conservative', *Harper's* (January 1983) quoted in Jonah Raskin, 'George Orwell and the Big Cannibal Critics', *Monthly Review* (May 1983), in *The Chetstnut Tree Cafe*.

395  Quoted in Malcolm Evans, 'Text Theory, Criticism: 20 Things You Never Knew about George Orwell', in Norris (ed.), p. 15.

396  Quoted in Evans in Norris (ed.), p. 16.

397  Crispin Aubrey, 'The Making of 1984', in Aubrey and Chilton (eds.), p. 13.

398  Bernard Crick, 'Orwell and English Socialism', in Peter Buitenhuis and Ira B. Nadel (eds.), *George Orwell: A Reassessment* (London: Macmillan, 1988), p. 19.

399  Patrick Reilly, *The Literature of Guilt from Gulliver to Golding* (Basingstoke: Macmillan, 1988), p. 99.

400  Conor Cruise O'Brien, *Observer* (31 December 1983), quoted in Bernard Crick, 'The Reception of *Nineteen Eighty-four*', in Kroes (ed.), p. 13.

401  Christopher Norris, 'Introduction', in Norris (ed.), p. 7.

402  Beatrix Campbell, 'Orwell – Paterfamilias or Big Brother?', in Norris (ed.), p. 131; Deirdre Beddoe, 'Hindrances and Help-Meets: Women in the Writings of George Orwell', in Norris (ed.), p. 153.

403  Daphne Patai, *The Orwell Mystique: A Study of Male Ideology* (Amherst: University of Massachusetts Press, 1984).

404  John Newsinger, *Orwells Politics* (Basingstoke: Macmillan, 1999), p. 8.

405  John Rodden, 'Orwell and the London Left Intelligentsia', in Holderness *et al.* (eds.), pp. 177–8.

406  Richard Rorty, *Contingency, Irony and Solidarity* (Cambridge: Cambridge University Press, 1989), p. 170.

404  Michael Walzer, *The Company of Critics: Social Criticism and Political Commitment in the Twentieth Century* (London: Halban, 1989), p. 135.

408 Shelden, p. 10.

409 Shelden, p. 484.

410 Peter Davison, *George Orwell: A Literary Life* (London: Macmillan, 1996), pp. 143–5.

411 Timothy Garton Ash, 'Orwell for Our Time', *Guardian* (5 May 2001).

412 Sean O'Casey, *Sunset and Evening Star* (London: 1954), pp. 133–5.

413 Jonathan Freedland, 'We're Watching It', *Guardian* (9 August 2000).

414 John Rossi, 'Orwell and Patriotism', *Contemporary Review* (August 1992), in *The Chestnut Cafe*.

415 This has been an implicit theme of Bernard Crick's work since the 1980s. See, for example, his introduction to Buitenhuis, Peter and Nadel, Ira, *George Orwell: A Reassessment* (Basingstoke: Macmillan, 1988).

416 Jeffrey Meyers, *Orwell: Wintry Conscience of a Generation* (New York WW Norton, 2000).

417 George Bush, speech to Congress, 20 September 2001.

418 George Orwell, 'In Defence of Comrade Zilliacus', late 1947/early 1948, in *CEJL*, Volume IV, p. 395.

419 Christopher Hitchens, *Orwell's Victory* (London: Allen Lane, 2002), p.350.

420 Rob Kroes, 'A Nineteen Eighty-Foreboding: Orwell and the Entropy of Politics', in Rob Kroes (ed.), *Nineteen Eighty-four and the Apocalyptic Imagination in America* (Amsterdam: Free University Press, 1985), p. 96.

421 Crick, p. 18.

422 Timothy Garton Ash, 'Orwell for Our Time', *Guardian* (5 May 2001).

423 George Orwell, review of John Galsworthy's *Glimpses and Reflections*, *New Statesman* (12 March 1938), in *CEJL*, Volume I, p. 307.

424 Orwell to Common, March 1938, in *CEJL*, Volume I, p. 310.

425 George Orwell, 'Lear, Tolstoy and the Fool', *Polemic* (March 1947) in *CEJL*, Volume IV, p. 290.

426 Orwell to Spender, 2 April 1938, in *CEJL*, Volume I, p.311.

427 Orwell to House, 11 April 1940, in *CEJL*, Volume I, p. 529.

428 Orwell diary, 27 April 1942, in *CEJL*, Volume II, p. 423.

429 George Orwell, 'The Prevention of Literature', *Polemic* (March 1946), in *CEJL*, Volume IV, pp. 59–72.

430 George Orwell, review of Jack Common's *The Freedom of the Streets*, *New English Weekly* (16 June 1938), in *CEJL*, Volume I, p. 335.

431 George Orwell, 'As I Please', *Tribune* (1 September 1944), in *CEJL*, Volume III, p. 224.

432 George Orwell, review of Osbert Sitwell's *Great Morning*, in *CEJL*, Volume IV, p. 443.

433 George Orwell, 'In Defence of P. G. Wodehouse', *Windmill* (July 1945), in *CEJL*, Volume III, p. 341; George Orwell, 'London Letter', *Partisan Review* (March–April 1942), p. 175; Orwell diary, 22 August 1940, in *CEJL*, Volume II, p. 367.

434 Orwell to Symons, 10 May 1948, in *CEJL*, Volume IV, p. 421.

435 Extracts from Orwell hospital notebook, 1949, in *CEJL*, Volume IV, p. 510.

436 Quoted in John Wain, 'In the Thirties', in Miriam Gross (ed.), *The World of George Orwell* (London: Weidenfeld and Nicolson, 1971), p. 83.

437 Crick, p. 408.

438 Malcolm Muggeridge, 'A Knight of the Woeful Countenance', in Gross (ed.), p. 172.

439 George Woodcock, *The Crystal Spirit: A Story of George Orwell* (London: Jonathan Cape, 1967), p. 22.

440 Woodcock, p. 24.

441 Quoted in John Coleman, 'The Critic of Popular Culture', in Gross (ed.), p. 101.

442 Orwell to Spender, quoted in Crick, p. 578.

443 Quoted in Shelden, p. 328.

444 Christopher Hitchens, *Letters to a Contrarian* (New York: Basic, 2001), p. 42.

# Chronology

## History

| | |
|---|---|
| 1903 | Bolshevik-Menshevik split in Russian Communist Party and pogroms against Jews. British suffragette movement begins. Panama Canal Zone granted to US to build and manage waterway. 28 May: Royal family of Serbia assassinated. 17 December: First controlled flight in heavier-than-air machine by Orville and Wilbur Wright at Kitty Hawk, US. |
| 1904 | 8 February: Russo-Japanese War begins. 1 May: Japanese victory at Yalu River. France and Britain sign Entente Cordiale. Photoelectric cell invented. |
| 1911 | Parliament Act curtails power of House of Lords, establishes five-yearly elections. Lloyd George's National Insurance Act. Moroccan crisis. Chinese Revolution. Ernest Rutherford discovers the nuclear model of the atom. 14 December: Roald Amundsen reaches South Pole. |
| 1917 | 12 March: Revolution in Russia. 6 April: US declares war on Germany, entering First World War. 9–14 April: Battle of Arras. 15 September: Russia proclaimed a republic. 6 November: Passchendaele captured by the British. 7 November: Bolshevik Revolution. 8 November: Balfour Declaration on Palestine as a 'national home' for the Jews. 15 December: Russo-German armistice signed. |
| 1921 | 14 October: Greece declares war on Turkey. 6 December: Irish Free State set up by Peace Treaty with Britain. |
| 1922 | 24 March: Four-Power Pacific Treaty ratified by US Senate. 2 July: Heavy fighting in Dublin, the Four Courts blown up. Aug–Sept: Defeat of Greek armies by the Turks. 28 October: Mussolini's Fascist 'March on Rome'. |

## Culture

Samuel Butler, *The Way of All Flesh*. Henry James, *The Ambassadors*. Rainer Maria Rilke, *Auguste Rodin*. Bertrand Russell, *Principles of Mathematics*. George Bernard Shaw, *Man and Superman*.

Anton Chekhov, *The Cherry Orchard*. Joseph Conrad, *Nostromo*. Giacomo Puccini, *Madama Butterfly*.

Conrad, *Under Western Eyes*. Thomas Mann, *Death in Venice*. Ezra Pound, *Canzoni*. Igor Stravinsky, *Petrushka*. Der Blaue Reiter group forms in Munich.

Guillaume Apollinaire, *Les Mamelles de Tirésias*. T S Eliot, *Prufrock*. D H Lawrence, *Look! We Have Come Through!*. W B Yeats, *The Wild Swans at Coole*.

Aldous Huxley, *Crome Yellow*. Lawrence, *Women in Love*. André Breton, *Les Champs magnétiques*.

Eliot, *The Waste Land*. James Joyce, *Ulysses*. Lawrence, *Aaron's Rod*. Osip Mandelstam, *Tristia*.

| Year | Age | Life |
|------|-----|------|
| 1924 | 21 | January: Takes up first provincial post at Myaungmya. Spring: Moves to Twante. |
| 1925 | 22 | January: Posted to Syriam, in charge of security at Burma Oil Company's refinery. October: Becomes Assistant Superintendent at police HQ at Insein. |
| 1926 | 23 | April: Moves to Moulmein. December: Takes up last post at Katha in the jungle of Upper Burma. |
| 1927 | 24 | July: Resigns from Indian Police on medical grounds. Winter: Goes 'down and out' in London's East End. |
| 1928 | 25 | Spring: Moves to cheap hotel in Paris, 6 rue du Pot de Fer. October: Publishes first article, 'La Censure en Angleterre' in *Le Monde*. December: First English article published, 'A Farthing Newspaper', in *G. K.'s Weekly*. |
| 1929 | 25 | Publishes articles in *Le Progrès civique*. August: Sends 'The Spike' to the *Adelphi*. October-December: All of his money is stolen. Gets a job as a dishwasher in a Paris hotel. December: Leaves Paris for his parents' home in Southwold, Suffolk. Jobs as a carer and tutor. |
| 1930 | 26 | April: Resumes tramping in London and Kent, Bedfordshire, Essex and Suffolk. October: Finishes 'A Scullion's Diary', the first version of *Down and Out in Paris and London*. |

| History | Culture |
|---|---|
| **1924** January: Ramsay MacDonald leads first Labour government. November: Conservative Party returns to office under Stanley Baldwin. | Bertolt Brecht, *The Threepenny Opera*. E M Forster, *A Passage to India*. Kafka, *The Hunger Artist*. Mann, *The Magic Mountain*. Breton, First Surrealist Manifesto. |
| **1925** 26 March: Hindenburg elected German president. 1 December: Treaty of Locarno signed in London. | John Dos Passos, *Manhattan Transfer*. F Scott Fitzgerald, *The Great Gatsby*. Adolf Hitler, *Mein Kampf*. Kafka, *The Trial*. Virginia Woolf, *Mrs Dalloway*. |
| **1926** 31 January: Evacuation of Cologne by British forces. General Strike in Britain. | Ernest Hemingway, *The Sun also Rises*. Lawrence, *The Plumed Serpent*. André Gide, *The Counterfeiters*. Kafka, *The Castle*. |
| **1927** Joseph Stalin comes to power. 21 May: Charles Lindbergh solo flight across Atlantic Ocean. | Forster, *Aspects of the Novel*. Hemingway, *Men without Women*. Franz Kafka, *Amerika*. Woolf, *To the Lighthouse*. Martin Heidegger, *Being and Time*. BBC public radio launched. |
| **1928** 9 June: Kingsford-Smith flies across the Pacific ocean. 18 July: Kellogg-Briand Pact for Peace accepted by Britain. 15 October: German airship with 60 passengers crosses Atlantic. Women in Britain enfranchised on same basis as men. Alexander Fleming discovers penicillin. | Aldous Huxley, *Point Counter Point*. Christopher Isherwood, *All the Conspirators*. D H Lawrence, *Lady Chatterley's Lover*. Erich Remarque, *All Quiet on the Western Front*. Woolf, *Orlando*. Yeats, *The Tower*. Maurice Ravel, *Boléro*. Kurt Weill, *The Threepenny Opera*. Walt Disney, *Steamboat Willie*. |
| **1929** Lateran Treaty. Yugoslavia under kings of Serbia. American slump and Wall Street crash. Young Plan for Germany. | Jean Cocteau, *Les Enfants Terribles*. William Faulkner, *The Sound and the Fury*. Robert Graves, *Good-bye to All That*. Ernest Hemingway, *A Farewell to Arms*. Woolf, *A Room of One's Own*. Salvador Dali and Luis Buñuel, *Un Chien andalou*. |
| **1930** Extreme parties (Communist and Nazi) win German elections: no majority can be found to form a government. London Maritime Disarmament Conference. Gandhi rebels against British Salt Monopoly and is imprisoned. | W H Auden, *Poems*. Eliot, *Ash Wednesday*. Faulkner, *As I Lay Dying*. Wyndham Lewis, *The Apes of God*. Evelyn Waugh, *Vile Bodies*. |

| 1931 | 27 | 'The Spike' appears in the *Adelphi* and is revised for inclusion in *Down and Out*. August-September: Hop-picking in Kent. October: 'Hop-picking' published in the *New Statesman*. December: Last time he goes 'down and out' in London. Tries and fails to get arrested. Moves from Paddington to Westminster. |
| 1932 | 29 | April: Takes up teaching post at Hawthorns School in Hayes, Middlesex. Leonard Moore becomes his agent. November: Chooses the pseudonym 'George Orwell'. |
| 1933 | 30 | *Down and Out in Paris and London* published in Britain (January) and the US (June). December: Completes revised manuscript of *Burmese Days*. Develops pneumonia and recovers in Southwold. |
| 1934 | 31 | October: Completes manuscript of *A Clergyman's Daughter*. Works in Booklovers' Corner, a bookshop in Hampstead, London. *Burmese Days* published in the US. |
| 1935 | 32 | March: *A Clergyman's Daughter* published in Britain. June: *Burmese Days* published in Britain. August: Shares a flat in Camden, London. |
| 1936 | 33 | January-March: Travels through northern England (the West Midlands, Lancashire and Yorkshire) researching *The Road to Wigan Pier*. April: Moves to a cottage in Wallington, Hertfordshire. *Keep the Aspidistra Flying* published in Britain. June: Marries Eileen O'Shaughnessy in Wallington. August: *A Clergyman's Daughter* published in the US. December: Delivers the manuscript of *The Road to Wigan Pier*. Leaves for Spain and joins the militia of POUM in the civil war. |
| 1937 | 34 | January: Involved in the siege of Huesca. March: *The Road to Wigan Pier* published in Britain, including a Left Book Club edition. May: Shot in the neck by a sniper in Spain. June: Discharged. Flees Spain. |
| 1938 | 35 | January: Completes manuscript of *Homage to Catalonia*. March: Goes to Prestoon Hall Sanatorium with tubercular lesion on left lung. April: *Homage to Catalonia* published in Britain. June: Joins the Independent Labour Party. September: Sails for Morocco with Eileen. December: Finishes draft of *Coming Up for Air*. |

| | History | Culture |
|---|---|---|
| 1931 | Great floods in China. Resignation of Labour government in Britain and formation of Coalition government under Ramsay MacDonald. | Faulkner, *Sanctuary*. Anthony Powell, *Afternoon Men*. Edmund Wilson, *Axel's Castle*. |
| 1932 | Kingdom of Saudi Arabia independent. Kingdom of Iraq independent. James Chadwick discovers neutron. | Auden, *The Orators*. Huxley, *Brave New World*. Jules Romains, *Les hommes de bonne volonté*. |
| 1933 | 30 January: Adolf Hitler appointed Chancellor and begins to establish supreme control. 27 February: German Reichstag set on fire. F D Roosevelt becomes US president; launches New Deal. | André Malraux, *La condition humaine*. Stephen Spender, *Poems*. Gertrude Stein, *The Autobiography of Alice B Toklas*. Nathanael West, *Miss Lonelyhearts*. |
| 1934 | 25 July: Dollfuss, Austrian Chancellor, murdered by Austrian Nazis. 2 August: Death of Hindenburg. Hitler becomes dictator. | Agatha Christie, *Murder on the Orient Express*. F Scott Fitzgerald, *Tender is the Night*. Henry Miller, *Tropic of Cancer*. |
| 1935 | 7 June: Stanley Baldwin succeeds Ramsay MacDonald as British prime minister. 3 October: War begins between Italy and Abyssinia. | Spender, *The Destructive Element*. George Gershwin, *Porgy and Bess*. Marx Brothers, *A Night at the Opera*. |
| 1936 | 20 January: Accession of King Edward VIII. 7 March: Repudiation of Locarno Treaty by Germany. 8 March: Remilitarisation of the Rhineland. 5 May: Italian troops occupy Addis Ababa. 18 July: Civil war breaks out in Spain. 10 December: In Britain Edward VIII abdicates after a reign of 325 days. Two days later, his brother, the Duke of York, becomes George VI. | Auden, *The Ascent of F6*. A J Ayer, *Language, Truth and Logic*. Huxley, *Eyeless in Gaza*. Sergey Prokofiev, *Peter and the Wolf*. BBC public television founded. |
| 1937 | 28 may: Coalition Ministry under Neville Chamberlain. 7 July: 'China incident': the Japanese begin attempted conquest of China. Arab-Jewish conflict in Palestine. | Auden, *Letters from Iceland*. Jean-Paul Sartre, *La Nausée*. John Steinbeck, *Of Mice and Men*. Pablo Picasso, *Guernica*. |
| 1938 | 13 March: Austria annexed by Germany (the Anschluss). 28 September: British Navy mobilised. Munich Crisis. 29 September: Munich Agreement between Chamberlain, Deladier, Hitler and Mussolini. In Germany, Jewish houses, synagogues, and schools are burnt down and shops looted (Kristallnacht). Otto Hahn and F Strassman discover nuclear fission. | Samuel Beckett, *Murphy*. Elizabeth Bowen, *The Death of the Heart*. Graham Greene, *Brighton Rock*. Waugh, *Scoop*. Sergey Eisenstein, *Alexander Nevsky*. |

1939   36   March: Returns to Wallington. *Coming up for Air* published.

1940   37   March: Publishes essay collection, *Inside the Whale*. May: Rents a flat near Baker Street, London. Becomes film and theatre critic of *Time and Tide*. June: Joins the Home Guard.

1941   38   February: *The Lion and the Unicorn* published. August: Joins the Empire Department of the BBC as head of cultural programming for India and south-east Asia.

| 1939 | May–September: Battle of Nomonhan between Japan and Soviet Union. 1 September: Germany invades Poland. 3 September: Britain and France declare war on Germany. 17 September: Soviet Union invades Poland. 30 November: Soviet Union invades Finland. | Joyce, *Finnegans Wake*. Ernst Jünger, *On the Marble Cliffs*. Spender, *The Still Centre*. |
|---|---|---|
| 1940 | 12 March: Finland capitulates. 9 April: Germany invades Denmark and Norway. 10 May: Germany invades Low Countries and France; Winston Churchill succeeds Chamberlain as British prime minister. 20 May: Germans reach English Channel. 28 May: Belgium capitulates. 27 May–4 June: Dunkirk. 10 June: Italy declares war. 10 July–15 September: Battle of Britain. 27 September: Tripartite Pact between Japan, Germany and Italy. 5 November: F D Roosevelt re-elected US president. Leon Trotsky assassinated in Mexico. | Auden, *Another Time*. Greene, *The Power and the Glory*. Hemingway, *For Whom the Bell Tolls*. Charlie Chaplin, *The Great Dictator*. Disney, *Fantasia*. |
| 1941 | 11 March: US Lease and Lend Bill signed by Roosevelt. 30 March: Rommel opens attack in North Africa. 11 April: Belgrade occupied by German forces. 27 May: German battleship, Bismark, sunk. 2 June: Clothes rationing begins in Britain. 18 June: Treaty of friendship between Turkey and Germany. 22 June: Germany attacks Russia. 19 September: Kiev entered by Germans. 6 October: Germany attacks Moscow. 16 October: Soviet government leaves Moscow. Odessa occupied by German and Rumanian troops. 14 November: Sinking of the Ark Royal. 1 December: Points rationing scheme in Britain. 4 December: German attack on Moscow halted. 7 December: Japanese attack on Pearl Harbor. US enters the Second World War. 10 December: Japan invades the Philippines. 25 December: Hong Kong surrenders to Japanese. | Auden, *New Year Letter*. Brecht, *Mother Courage and her Children*. Orson Welles, *Citizen Kane*. |

| | | |
|---|---|---|
| 1943 | 40 | November: Begins *Animal Farm*. Resigns from the BBC and becomes Literary Editor of *Tribune*, writing weekly column 'As I Please'. |
| 1944 | 41 | February: Completes first draft of *Animal Farm*. June: With Eileen, adopts a son, Richard Horatio Blair. |
| 1945 | 42 | March: Leaves *Tribune*, becoming a war correspondent for the *Observer*. Eileen dies suddenly. August: *Animal Farm* published. |
| 1946 | 43 | *Animal Farm* published in the US. May: Begins spending part of the year in a cottage on the Scottish island of Jura, Inner Hebrides. November: Resumes 'As I Please' column. |

## History

| Culture |
|---|

**1943**  18 January: German army in retreat.
Siege of Leningrad ends. 27 January:
American bombers attack Germany. 31
January: Remnants of German army
outside Stalingrad surrender. 5 July:
Battle of Kursk begins.25 July: Mussolini
overthrown. 28 July: Italian Fascist Party
dissolved. 7 September: Italy surrenders.
10 September: Germany seizes Rome.
6 November: Russians take Kiev.
28 November: Tehran Conference.

Eliot, *The Four Quartets*. Sartre,
*Being and Nothingness*. Richard
Rodgers and Oscar
Hammerstein, *Oklahoma!*

**1944**  4 June: Allied forces enter Rome. 6 June:
D-Day: Allied invasion of Europe. 20
July: 'Bomb plot' on Hitler's life. 1 August:
Warsaw uprising. 15 August: Allied forces
land in southern France. 25 August: Paris
liberated. 3 October: Germany crushes
Warsaw rising.

Auden, *For the Time Being*. Jorge
Luis Borges, *Fictions*. Eisenstein,
*Ivan the Terrible*. Laurence Olivier,
*Henry V*.

**1945**  12 January: General Russian offensive
begins. 4–12 February: Yalta Conference.
13–14 February: Dresden raids. 12 April:
Death of F D Roosevelt. 13 April:
Russians enter Vienna. 16 April: Last
Russian offensive begins. 28 April: Death
of Mussolini. 30 April: Death of Hitler.
2 May: Berlin in Russian hands.
7 May: Germans surrender at Reims.
9 May: Russians enter Prague. 17 July:
Potsdam Conference. 26 July: Labour
Party wins general election; Clement
Attlee becomes prime minister.
6 August: Atomic bomb destroys
Hiroshima. 14 August: Unconditional
surrender of Japan. 27 December:
IMF and World Bank established.

Waugh, *Brideshead Revisited*. Karl
Popper, *The Open Society and Its
Enemies*. Benjamin Britten, *Peter
Grimes*. Unesco founded.

**1946**  5 March: Churchill's 'Iron Curtain'
speech. Cold War begins. 18 April: End of
League of Nations. 13 July: £937m US loan
to Britain. 22 July: King David Hotel,
British HQ in Jerusalem, blown up. 1
August: Paris Peace Conference. 16
October: Nuremberg sentences carried
out: Goering's suicide. 23 October:
General Assembly of the United Nations
(UN) opens in New York.

Bertrand Russell, *History of
Western Philosophy*. Sartre,
*Existentialism and Humanism*.
Eugene O'Neill, *The Iceman
Cometh*. Cocteau,
*La Belle et la Bête*.

| Year | Age | Life |
|------|-----|------|
| 1947 | 44 | October: Bedridden with tuberculosis, weeks after finishing first draft of *Nineteen Eighty-four*. December: Enters a hospital near Glasgow. |
| 1948 | 45 | February: Begins experimental treatment with new drug, streptomycin. July: Discharged and returns to Jura. November: Completes revised draft of *Nineteen Eighty-four*. |
| 1949 | 46 | January: Enters Cotswold Sanatorium, Gloucestershire. March-April: Provides the Information Research Department with a list of 36 'suspect' individuals. June: *Nineteen Eighty-four* published in Britain and the US. September: Moves to University College Hospital, London. October: Marries Sonia Bronwell. |
| 1950 | 46 | 21 January: Dies from a lung haemorrhage. Buried in a churchyard in Sutton Courtenay, Oxfordshire. |

| History | Culture |
|---|---|
| 1947 | 5 June: Marshall Plan inaugurated. 15 August: India and Pakistan become independent and separate states. 6 October: International organisation of Communist Parties (Cominform) set up. 14 October: Sound barrier broken. 15 December: 'Big Four' talks on Germany break down. | Primo Levi, *If This Is a Man.* Mann, *Doctor Faustus.* Robert Lowell wins Pulitzer Prize. |
| 1948 | 4 January: Burma independent. 30 January: Gandhi assassinated. 27 February: Communists seize power in Czechoslovakia. 14 May: British mandate in Palestine ended; new State of Israel proclaimed. 1 July: Berlin airlift. 5 July: British National Health Service inaugurated. 1 August: Economic union of French, US and British zones in Germany. 4 September: North Korea independent, following South Korea. 17 September: UN mediator in Palestine assassinated. 3 November: Harry S Truman elected US president. 10 December: UN adopts Declaration of Human Rights. | Auden, *The Age of Anxiety.* Brecht, *The Caucasian Chalk Circle.* Greene, *The Heart of the Matter.* Norman Mailer, *The Naked and the Dead.* Alan Paton, *Cry, the Beloved Country.* Vittorio De Sica, *Bicycle Thieves.* |
| 1949 | 4 April: 12 nations sign the North Atlantic Treaty, creating Nato. 18 April: Republic of Ireland proclaimed. 23 May: Federal Republic of Germany (FDR) proclaimed. 14 September: Konrad Adenaur becomes first chancellor of FDR. 21 September: Soviet Union tests atom bomb. 1 October: People's Republic of China proclaimed under Chairman Mao Zedong. 12 October: German Democratic Republic proclaimed in Soviet sector. Stereophonic sound invented. First successful kidney transplant. | Nelson Algren, *The Man with the Golden Arm.* Simone de Beauvoir, *The Second Sex.* Arthur Miller, *Death of a Salesman.* Ralph Vaughan Williams, *An Oxford Elegy.* |
| 1950 | 26 January: Indian republic proclaimed under President Rajendra Prasad. 14 February: Soviet Union–China alliance signed. 25 June: North Korea invades South Korea. Korean War begins; US supports South Korea. 19 October: China invades Tibet. | Pablo Neruda, *Canto General.* Eugène Ionesco, *The Bald Prima Donna.* Billy Wilder, *Sunset Boulevard.* |

# List of Works

BOOKS

*Down and Out in Paris and London* (London: Victor Gollancz, 1933)
*Burmese Days* (London: Victor Gollancz, 1935)
*A Clergyman's Daughter* (London: Victor Gollancz, 1935)
*Keep the Aspidistra Flying* (London: Victor Gollancz, 1936)
*The Road to Wigan Pier* (London: Victor Gollancz, 1937)
*Homage to Catalonia* (London: Secker and Warburg, 1938)
*Coming Up for Air* (London: Victor Gollancz, 1939)
*The Lion and the Unicorn* (London: Secker and Warburg, 1941)
*The English People* (London: Collins, 1942)
*Betrayal of the Left* (London: Victor Gollancz, 1945)
*Animal Farm* (London: Secker and Warburg, 1945)
*Nineteen Eighty-four* (London: Secker and Warburg, 1949)

JOURNALISM

'On Kipling's Death' (23 January 1936) in *New English Weekly*
'Shooting an Elephant' (Autumn 1936) *New Writing*
'Spilling the Spanish Beans' (29 July and 2 September 1937)
    *New English Weekly*
'Why I Joined the Independent Labour Party', (24 June 1938) *New Leader*
'Not Counting Niggers' (July 1939), *Adelphi*
'Marrakech' (Christmas 1939) *New Writing*
'Boys' Weeklies' (March 1940) *Horizon*
'Inside the Whale' (London: Victor Gollancz: 1940), *Inside the Whale*
'Charles Reade' (17 August 1940) *New Statesman and Nation*
'My Country, Right or Left' (Autumn 1940) *Folios of New Writing*
'Rudyard Kipling' (February 1942) *Horizon*
'Raffles and Miss Blandish' (October 1944) *Horizon*
'Notes on Nationalism' (October 1945) *Polemic*
'You and the Atom Bomb' (19 October 1945) *Tribune*
'The Prevention of Literature' (March 1946) *Polemic*

'Second Thoughts on James Burnham' (May 1946) *Polemic*

'Politics v. Literature: An Examination of *Gulliver's Travels*',
    (September – October 1946) *Polemic*

'Riding Down from Bangor' (22 November 1946) *Tribune*

'Arthur Koestler' (1946) *Focus*

'Toward European Unity' (July – August 1947) *Partisan Review*

'Writers and Leviathan' (Summer 1948) *Politics and Letters*

'Britain's Struggle for Survival: The Labor Government After Three
    Years', *Commentary* (October 1948)

'Reflections on Gandhi' (January 1949) *Partisan Review*


COLUMNS

'London Letter' (January 1942 – Summer 1946) *Partisan Review*

'As I Please' (December 1943 – February 1945 and November 1946 –
    April 1947) *Tribune*

# Further Reading

BIBLIOGRAPHIES AND CATALOGUES

Fenwick, Gillian, *George Orwell: A Bibliography* (Winchester, United Kingdom: St Paul's Bibliographies, 1998).

Meyers, Jeffrey, 'George Orwell: A Bibliography.' *Bulletin of Bibliography* (July–September 1974): 117–21.

——, 'George Orwell: A Selected Checklist.' *Modern Fiction Studies* (Spring 1975): 133–6.


BIOGRAPHIES AND MEMOIRS

*Books*

Alldritt, Keith, *The Making of George Orwell* (London: Edward Arnold, 1969): a book critical of Orwell's literary qualities.

Atkins, John, *George Orwell* (London: Calder and Boyars, 1954): one of the first eulogies.

Brander, Laurence, *George Orwell* (London: Longmans, Green, and Company, 1954).

Buddicom, Jacintha, *Eric and Us: A Remembrance of George Orwell* (London: Leslie Frewin, 1974): a recollection by a childhood friend of Eric Blair.

Coppard, Audrey and Crick, Bernard (eds.), *Orwell Remembered* (London: Ariel Books, 1984): collection of eyewitness accounts and essays about Orwell.

Crick, Bernard, *George Orwell: A Life* (London: Secker and Warburg, 1980. Reprinted by Harmondsworth: Penguin, 1982): the best-known biography, bordering on hagiography, of Orwell.

Fyvel, T R, *George Orwell: A Personal Memoir* (London: Weidenfeld and Nicolson, 1982): recollections of Orwell's colleague at *Tribune* and fellow anti-communist activist.

Gross, Miriam (ed.), *The World of George Orwell* (London: Weidenfeld and Nicolson, 1971): wide-ranging collection of observations and interpretations of Orwell from earliest days to his death.

Hollis, Christopher, *A Study of George Orwell: The Man and His Works* (London: Hollis and Carter, 1956): a testament to the greatness of Orwell.

Hopkinson, Tom, *George Orwell* (London: Longman, 1953).

Lewis, Peter, *George Orwell: The Road to 1984* (New York: Harcourt Brace, 1981).

Meyers, Jeffrey. *Orwell: Wintry Conscience of a Generation* (New York: W W Norton, 2000): the outcome of 30 years' study, a book which reinforces the standard narrative.

Rees, Richard, *George Orwell: Fugitive from the Camp of Victory* (London: Secker and Warburg, 1961): observations of Orwell's friend, patron and literary executor.

Shelden, Michael, *Orwell: The Authorised Biography* (London: Heinemann, 1991): thorough in research and scope, but limited in conclusions.

Stansky, Peter and Abrahams, William, *The Unknown Orwell* (London: Constable, 1972) and *Orwell: The Transformation* (London: Constable, 1979): provocative two-volume study reassessing the 'making' of Orwell.

Thompson, John, *Orwell's London* (London: Fourth Estate, 1984).

Wadhams, Stephen, *Remembering Orwell* (Markham, Ontario: Penguin Books Canada, 1984).

Woodcock, George, *The Crystal Spirit: A Study of George Orwell* (London: Jonathan Cape, 1967): dynamic study by a literary contemporary of Orwell's.

## Book Sections and Articles

Dunn, Avril, 'My Brother, George Orwell'. *Twentieth Century* (March 1961): 255–61.

Fen, Elisaveta, 'George Orwell's First Wife.' *Twentieth Century* (August 1960): 115–26: one of the only studies of Eileen Blair.

Fyvel, T R, 'A Case for George Orwell?' *Twentieth Century* (September 1956): 256–9.

——, 'George Orwell and Eric Blair: Glimpses of a Dual Life.' *Encounter* (July 1959): 60–5.

Heppenstall, Rayner, 'Orwell Intermittent.' *Twentieth Century* (May 1955): 470–83: recollections of Orwell's flatmate, a fellow writer.

——, *Four Absentees* (London: Barrie and Rockcliff, 1960).

Warburg, Fredric, *An Occupation for Gentlemen* (London: Hutchinson, 1959): memoir by Orwell's publisher.

Woodcock, George, 'George Orwell, Nineteenth-century Liberal,' *Politics* (December 1946), 384–8.

——, *The Writer and Politics* (London: Porcupine, 1948).

——, 'Recollections of George Orwell.' *Northern Review* (August-September 1953): 18.

*World Review* (June 1950). Special edition on Orwell with contributions from T R Fyvel, Tom Hopkinson, Stephen Spender and others.

## Television

'Orwell Remembered.' *Arena*, 3 parts. British Broadcasting Corporation, 1984. Produced by Nigel Williams.

'The Road to the Left.' *Omnibus*. British Broadcasting Corporation, 1970. Produced by Melvyn Bragg.

## Radio

'George Orwell: A Programme of Recorded Reminiscences.' British Broadcasting Corporation, 1960. Produced by Rayner Heppenstall.

'George Orwell: A Radio Biography.' Canadian Broadcasting Corporation, January 1984. Developed by Stephen Wadhams. Narrated by George Woodcock.

CRITICAL STUDIES

## Books

Aubrey, Crispin and Chilton, Paul (eds.), *Nineteen Eighty-four in 1984* (London: Comedia, 1983): 'update' of Orwell's work, considering contemporary issues such as technology and propaganda.

Bal, Sant Singh, *George Orwell: The Ethical Imagination*. Delhi: Arnold-Heinemann, 1981.

Bloom, Harold (ed.), *George Orwell*. New York: Chelsea House, 1987.

Buitenhuis, Peter and Nadel, Ira (eds.), *George Orwell: A Reassessment* (Basingstoke, UK: Macmillan, 1988): a collection that is more of a reaffirmation than a reassessment.

Calder, Jenni, *Chronicles of Conscience* (London: Secker and Warburg, 1968): a comparative study of Orwell and Arthur Koestler.

——, *Huxley and Orwell: Brave New World and Nineteen Eighty-Four* (London: Edward Arnold, 1976).

——, *Animal Farm & Nineteen Eighty-Four* (Milton Keynes, UK: Open University Press, 1987).

Connelly, Mark, *The Diminished Self: Orwell and the Loss of Freedom* (Pittsburgh: Duquesne University Press, 1987).

Crick, Bernard (ed.), *George Orwell: Nineteen Eighty-four* (Oxford: Clarendon, 1984).

Davison, Peter, *George Orwell: A Literary Life* (Basingstoke, UK: Macmillan, 1996): slim volume complementing the 20-volume set of Orwell's writings catalogued by Davison.

Edelheit, Steven, *Dark Prophecies* (New York: Revisionist Press, 1979).

Fowler, Roger, *The Language of George Orwell* (London: Macmillan, 1995): one of the few book-length examinations of Orwell's use of language.

Freedman, Carl, *George Orwell: A Study in Ideology and Literary Form* (New York: Garland, 1988).

Hitchens, Christopher, *Orwell's Victory* (London: Allen Lane, 2002): vehement, sometimes mean-spirited, appropriation of Orwell by a would-be successor.

Holderness, Graham, Loughrey, Bryan, and Yousaf, Naham (eds.), *George Orwell* (London: Macmillan, 1998): a provocative collection of assessments of Orwell from a variety of political and cultural angles.

Howe, Irving, *1984 Revisited: Totalitarianism in Our Century* (London: Harper & Row, 1983): ongoing work of prominent American 'liberal' publishing on Orwell since 1950s.

——, *Orwell's 'Nineteen Eighty-four': Text, Sources, Criticism* (New York: Harcourt, Brace and World, 1963).

Huber, Peter, *Orwell's Revenge: The 1984 Palimpsest* (New York: Free Press, 1994).

Hunter, Lynette, *George Orwell: The Search for a Voice* (Milton Keynes: Open University Press, 1984): excellent literary and cultural critique of Orwell's works.

Kalechofsky, Roberta, *George Orwell* (New York: Frederick Unger, 1973).

Kubal, David, *George Orwell's Art and Politics* (Notre Dame, Indiana: University of Notre Dame Press, 1972).

Lee, Robert Alan, *Orwell's Fiction* (Notre Dame, Indiana: University of Notre Dame Press, 1969).

Lief, Ruth Ann, *Homage to Oceania: The Prophetic Vision of George Orwell* (Columbus: Ohio State University Press, 1969).

Meyers, Jeffrey (ed.), *George Orwell: The Critical Heritage* (London: Routledge and Kegan Paul, 1975): collection of contemporary reviews of Orwell's books.

——, *A Reader's Guide to George Orwell* (London: Thames and Hudson, 1975).

Meyers, Jeffrey and Meyers, Valerie, *An Annotated Bibliography of Criticism* (New York: Garland, 1977).

Meyers, Valerie, *George Orwell* (London: Macmillan, 1991).

Mulvihill, Robert (ed.), *Reflections on America, 1984* (Athens: University of Georgia Press, 1986): record of one of the 1984 conferences on Orwell.

Newsinger, John, *Orwell's Politics* (London: Macmillan, 1999): strident defence, especially against 'feminist' and 'left' critics, of Orwell.

Norris, Christopher (ed.), *Inside the Myth: Orwell, Views from the Left* (London: Lawrence and Wishart, 1984): perhaps the most interesting of the 1984 collections, with criticisms of Orwell's treatment of politics, economics, history and gender.

Oldsey, Bernard and Browne, Joseph (eds.), *Critical Essays on George Orwell* (Boston: G K Hall, 1986).

Patai, Daphne, *The Orwell Mystique: A Study in Male Ideology* (Amherst: University of Massachusetts Press, 1984): challenge to Orwell's treatment of women in his life and in his writing.

Plank, Robert, *George Orwell's Guide through Hell: A Psychological study of Nineteen Eighty-four.* (San Bernardino, California: Burgo Press, 1986).

Rai, Alok, *Orwell and the Politics of Despair* (Cambridge: Cambridge University Press, 1988): a challenge to Orwell offering a contrast to the standard portrayal of the author's 'positive' ideas and life.

Reilly, Patrick, *George Orwell: The Age's Adversary* (London: Macmillan, 1986): thoughtful, generally supportive study of Orwell as an honourable dissenter.

Rodden, John, *The Politics of Literary Reputation: The Making and Claiming of 'St George' Orwell* (New York: Oxford University Press, 1989): interesting study of the politics around Orwell.

Sandison, Alan, *The Last Man in Europe: An Essay on George Orwell* (London: Macmillan, 1974).

Slater, Ian, *Orwell: The Road to Airstrip One* (London: Norton, 1985).

Small, Christopher, *The Road to Miniluv: George Orwell, the State, and God* (London: Gollancz, 1975).

Smyer, Richard, *Primal Dream and Primal Crime: Orwell's Development as a Psychological Novelist* (Columbia: University of Missouri Press, 1979).

Steinhoff, William, *The Road to 1984* (London: Weidenfeld and Nicolson, 1975).

Wemyss, Courtney and Ugrinsky, Alexej, *George Orwell* (New York: Greenwood, 1987).

West, W J, *The Larger Evils: Nineteen Eighty-four: The Truth Behind the Satire* (Edinburgh: Canongate, 1992).

Williams, Raymond, *Orwell* (Glasgow: Fontana, 1971): slim but influential booklet re-shaping the analysis of 'Orwell' as the construction of both the author and his admirers.

—— (ed.), *George Orwell: A Collection of Critical Essays* (Englewood Cliffs, New Jersey: Prentice-Hall, 1974).

Young, John Wesley, *Orwell's Newspeak and its Nazi and Communist Antecedents* (Charlottesville: University Press of Virginia, 1991).

Zwerdling, Alex, *Orwell and the Left* (New Haven: Yale University Press, 1974).

## Book Sections and Articles

Deutscher, Isaac, '1984 – The Mysticism of Cruelty' in *Heretics and Renegades* (London: Hamish Hamilton, 1955): a breakthrough study of the book and the Cold War.

Hitchens, Christopher, *Unacknowledged Legislation: Writers in the Public Sphere* (London: Verso, 2001): an essay on Orwell more notable for its sustained attack on Raymond Williams.

Leavis, Q D, 'The Literary Life Respectable: Mr. George Orwell.' *Scrutiny* (September 1940): 173–6: the first comprehensive review of Orwell and his work.

O'Brien, Conor Cruise, *Writers and Politics* (New York: Pantheon, 1965): intriguing approach by an author who criticises the use of 'Orwell' by Cold Warriors.

Pritchett, V S, 'George Orwell' in Gilbert Phelps (ed.), *Living Writers: Being Critical Studies Broadcast in the BBC Third Programme* (London: Sylvan Press, 1949).

Savage, D S, 'The Fatalism of George Orwell' in Boris Ford (ed.), *The New Penguin Guide to English Literature*, Volume 8 (Harmondsworth: Penguin, 1983).

Trilling, Lionel, 'George Orwell and the Politics of Truth' in *The Opposing Self* (London: Secker and Warburg, 1955): a landmark essay constructing Orwell as the icon for the 'vital center' of Cold War America.

Walton, David, 'George Orwell and Antisemitism.' *Patterns of Prejudice* (1982): 19–34.

Orwell Archive, University College, London
**www.ucl.ac.uk/library/special-coll/orwell.htm**
In 1960, Orwell's widow, Sonia Brownell, gave the author's
manuscripts, notebooks and personal effects to the college. These have
been supplemented by donations, purchases and loans from the British
Broadcasting Corporation to create a research centre for Orwell studies,
'by bringing together all [Orwell's] printed works, including newspaper
items; private correspondence; other private papers in the possession
of his widow; printed matter other than his own which will help later
generations to understand the controversies in which he was involved;
and tape recordings or written statements by all with first hand
experience of him of any consequence'.

British Broadcasting Corporation Archive, Caversham
The BBC holds written material relating to Orwell's programmes for the
World Service from 1941 to 1943.

# Picture Sources

The author and publishers wish to express their thanks to the following sources of illustrative material and/or permission to reproduce it. They will make proper acknowledgements in future editions in the event that any omissions have occurred.

Peter Blake: p. 130; Hulton Archive: p. 137; Penguin Books: p. 45; Topham Picturepoint: pp. 11, 16, 22, 26, 36, 42, 43, 55, 59, 62, 75, 82, 96, 104, 107; University College, London: pp. xi, xii, 3, 6, 8, 19, 33, 51, 64, 86, 90, 114, 121, 124.

# Index

Labour Party, 68–9, 74, 93, 103; fall of government (1931), 35, 37; General Election victory (1945), 75–6; history, 69
language, Orwell's concern with, 77, 98, 129
Laski, Harold, 35, 88, 90, 108, 111
Leavis, Q D, 58
Left Book Club, 14, 34, 40, 54; history, 34
*Left Review*, 44
Lenin, 92
liberalism, 57, 58, 94, 112, 128, 138
*Life*, 103
Liverpool, slum clearance in, 38
London, 10, 13, 16, 64, 85; East End, 10; materialism of, 27–8; Orwell's literary circle in, 89; Hyde Park, 93; depicted in *Nineteen Eighty-four*, 95, 101; University College Hospital, 114
London, Jack, 6, 10
Lyons, Eugene, 91

McCarthy, Mary, 91
McCarthy, Senator Joseph, 100, 109
Macdonald, Dwight, 83, 91, 111
Mackenzie, Compton, 30
McNair, John, 46
Mailer, Norman, 70
Malraux, André, 90
*Manchester Evening News*, 68, 72
*Manchester Guardian*, 17–18
Mao Zedong, 100
Marshall Plan, 99, 113
Martin, Kingsley, 84
Marx, Karl, 35, 81; biography, 35
Marx (dog), 133
Marxism, 41, 57; Marxist English, 78
mass culture, 28
materialism, viii, 27–8, 49
Matthews, Herbert, 120
May, Alan Nunn, 110
Mayberry, George, 120
Meyer, Michael, 90
Meyers, Jeffrey, 131
middle class, 39, 40, 59, 61, 63
Miller, Henry, 55–6; biography, 55
Milosz, Czeslaw, 119
Milton, John, 65
Ministry of Information, 64, 79–80
*Modern Youth*, 13
Moore, Leonard, 14, 15, 18, 26
Morton, A L, 120
Mosley, Oswald, 37, 39; biography, 38
Motihari, 1

Muggeridge, Malcolm, 21, 65, 90, 135
Mulvihill, Robert, 125
Murry, John Middleton, 9
Mussolini, Benito, 42, 52

*Nation*, 120
National Unemployed Workers' Movement (NUWM), 38
nationalism, 7, 87
Nato, 113
Nehru, Jawaharlal 'Pandit', 22
*New English Weekly*, 44
*New Leader*, 91, 109
*New Republic*, 120
*New Statesman*, 13, 43, 44, 45, 46, 66, 84, 97
*New York Times*, 103
Newsinger, John, 127
Nietzsche, Friedrich Wilhelm, 74
Norris, Christopher, 127
nostalgia, 52

O'Brien, Conor Cruise, 122, 126
O'Casey, Sean, 130
O'Shaughnessy, Eileen, 32, 33, 41, 43, 50, 64; death, 86
*Observer*, 45, 68, 86, 126
Orwell, George (Eric Arthur Blair): character, viii, 28; 'George Orwell' persona, 1, 2, 6, 7, 9, 11, 14–15, 57, 116, 117, 123, 124, 136, 138–9; childhood, 2–7; class prejudices, 3; attitude to women, 3–4; schooldays, 4–7, 94; police service in Burma, 7–9; moves to Paris, 10; journalism, 11–13, 64, 68; experience of poverty, 12–13, 17; political development, 18, 29, 35, 47–51, 56–7, 66, 73, 76, 89–90; early courtship, 18–19; attitude towards imperialism, 20–23, 24; pacifism, 23–4, 51, 54, 66–7; ill health, 24, 50, 64, 87, 94–5, 106, 114–15; relationship with Kay Welton, 27; daily schedule, 27; commitment to socialism, 29, 35, 49, 50, 60, 73, 89, 115, 124, 134, 136; marriage to Eileen O'Shaughnessy, 32, 41; and the working-class, 33–4, 36–7, 38–40, 73, 104–5, 127, 135–6; attack on socialists, 38–9; difficulties with socialism, 40, 46, 57, 59, 67, 68, 75, 88, 112, 114, 119; and Spanish Civil War, 41–50; breach with the 'Left', 43, 110; joins Independent Labour Party, 46, 51; liberalism, 57, 58, 94, 112, 128, 138; abandons pacifism, 58,

60, 62, 66; patriotism, 59, 62, 87–8; radio broadcasts, 65–6, 77; pessimism, 68, 76, 92, 113, 135; *Tribune* literary editor, 69–70, 78; 'As I Please' column, 69–74, 77, 85, 87, 90, 93; cultural commentator, 70–74, 117; connection with British intelligence, 74, 105, 122, 129, 136; surprised by Labour's election victory, 75–6; concern with language, 77–8, 98, 129; difficulty publishing *Animal Farm*, 79–80, 82; emotional instability, 87; developing anti-communism, 89–94, 111, 136; final breach with socialism, 103; compiles list of communist sympathisers, 105–10, 136; favours European integration, 112–13; marriage to Sonia Brownell, 114, 116; death, 115; posthumous tributes, 117–18; sense of irony, 133
WORKS: *Animal Farm*, vii, 46, 78–85, 86, 95, 101, 105, 115–16, 118; 'Boys' Weeklies', 70–71; *Burmese Days*, 8, 9, 18, 19–22, 24, 27, 29; *A Clergyman's Daughter*, 5, 13, 25–7, 30, 31, 98; *Coming Up for Air*, 2, 52–5, 98, 125; *Down and Out in Paris and London*, 11–18, 20, 24, 29, 30, 40, 80; 'A Hanging', 13, 21; *Homage to Catalonia*, viii, 43, 45–50, 61, 66, 67, 90, 118, 120, 121, 134; 'Hop-Picking', 13; 'Inside the Whale', 55, 56, 92; *Inside the Whale*, 58, 70; 'James Burnham and the Managerial Revolution', 89; *Keep the Aspidistra Flying*, 18, 27–30, 53, 58; 'Letter from London', 76; *The Lion and the Unicorn*, viii–ix, 60–62, 104; 'Literature and the Left', 77; 'My Country, Right or Left', 59, 62; 'New Words', 77; *Nineteen Eighty-four*, vii, 5, 18, 47, 53, 54, 73, 76, 94–9, 101–5, 112, 116, 117, 119, 120, 122, 125, 126, 129, 136; 'Not Counting Niggers', 23; 'Notes on Nationalism', 87; 'On Kipling's Death', 22; 'Politics and the English Language', 88; 'Politics and Literature', 89; 'Politics v. Literature: An Examination of *Gulliver's Travels*', 88; 'The Prevention of English Literature', 88; 'Raffles and Miss Blandish', 85; *The Road to Wigan Pier*, viii, 29, 33–40, 41, 46, 53, 61, 73; 'Romance', 9; 'Shooting the Elephant', 21–2; 'The Spike', 12; 'Spilling the Spanish Beans', 44;

'Struggle for Survival', 113; 'Such, Such Were the Joys', 4, 94; 'Toward European Unity', 112; 'Why I Write', 89, 134; 'Writers and Leviathan', 112; 'You and the Atom Bomb', 102
Orwell Archive, 109, 123

pacifism, x, 7, 23, 45, 51, 54, 66–7, 74, 87; Orwell rejects, 58, 60, 62, 66
Paris, 10, 12, 13; Latin Quarter, 11; Montmartre, 17
*Partisan Review*, 66, 67, 68, 90, 91, 93, 94, 103, 109
Patai, Daphne, 127
patriotism, 59, 62, 87–8, 131
Peters, Richard, 119
Pitter, Ruth, 10
Podhoretz, Norman, 125; quoted, 117
Poland, 119
*Polemic*, 88
popular culture, 70–72
POUM, 41, 42–3, 45, 48, 49, 67, 92
poverty, 17, 33, 34, 73, 134
Powell, Anthony, 90; on Orwell, 120
power, 97, 102
Priestley, J B, 15, 107
Pritchett, V S, 25, 26, 45, 97, 118
*Progrès civique*, 11, 21
propaganda, 49, 76–7, 81, 95; anti-communist, vii, viii, 106
psychological warfare, 91, 92, 108

Rahv, Philip, 90, 91, 103
Read, Herbert, 46, 51
Reade, Charles, 58; biography, 59
Redgrave, Michael, 106, 107
Rees, Sir Richard, 13, 29–30, 68; biography, 30; on *Animal Farm* and *Nineteen Eighty-four*, 104–5; and Orwell's list, 106, 109, 110; tribute to Orwell, 121
Reilly, Patrick, 126
religion, 7; in Spain, 48
Robeson, Paul, 107
Rodden, John, 127
Roosevelt, Eleanor, 109
Rorty, Richard, 128
Rossi, John, 131
Russia, *see* Soviet Union
Rutherford, Mark (William Hale White), 70; biography, 71

Schlesinger, Arthur, Jr, 94, 108, 109
Secker and Warburg, 41, 95
Second World War, 23, 56, 76, 85, 89, 92, 105, 138